Mother Teresa of Calcutta
A Personal Portrait

Fr. Leo Maasburg

Translated by Michael J. Miller

ABRIDGED EDITION

Ignatius Press–Augustine Institute
San Francisco   Greenwood Village, CO

Ignatius Press Distribution
P.O. Box 1339
Fort Collins, CO 80522
Tel: (800) 651-1531
www.ignatius.com

Augustine Institute
6160 S. Syracuse Way, Suite 310
Greenwood Village, CO 80111
Tel: (866) 767-3155
www.augustineinstitute.org

Cover Design: Devin Schadt

Cover Art: *Saint Mother Teresa*
By Gabrielle Schadt, Copyright © 2016

Contents

ACKNOWLEDGMENTS

My heartfelt thanks go to Mr. Stephan Baier for his professional, sympathetic collaboration in writing this book, and his efficient coordination of the many individual steps that were necessary to produce it. My great thanks also go to his understanding family.

I also sincerely thank Mrs. Barbara Polak for her meticulous and speedy transcription of the text.

My deep gratitude goes to Mr. Michael J. Miller and to my cousin Alix Henley for the beautiful translation of the book into the English language.

PREFACE

What Would She Want?

MOTHER TERESA is one of the truly great and influential personages of the twentieth century. She is, as even unbelievers and critics readily admit, an outstanding figure in the history of our times and in Church history. Above all, however, she was and remains a fascinating woman. I see this in the shining eyes of the many people who, as soon as they learn that I was privileged to work closely with Mother Teresa for several years, ask me to tell them something about her.

Why are modern people of the twenty-first century interested in a saintly woman of the twentieth century whom they themselves never met? In our hectic, fast-paced era that rushes from one fashion to the next, what can possibly be so interesting and inspiring about a religious Sister who, when a critic impertinently remarked that she was two hundred years behind in her theology, smiled and replied, "No, two thousand years!"?

On the numerous trips on which I was able to accompany Mother Teresa during her later years, I experienced something of the radiance and fascination of her personality. For our media world, which craves celebrities of every sort, she was an extraordinary, irreplaceable, shining "star"—surrounded not by the rich and the beautiful but rather by the poorest of the poor, the deformed, the outcasts of society. She was a forceful, shrewd, charismatic and humble personality who did not try to dominate but wanted to serve, and she was an innovative character whose greatest visible success was the fact that, through her works and example, so many young women throughout the world cheerfully joined the ranks of Jesus' disciples and thereby found the meaning of their lives. Many men and women of all generations allowed themselves to be inspired by Mother Teresa's love for Jesus. She was a "star" who was a reluctant public figure yet used publicity quite effectively for her cause.

Mother Teresa never made herself the center of attention. But when she was put in the spotlight by others—after she was awarded the Nobel Peace Prize in 1979—that was practically a perpetual state. She used the opportunity to point attention away from herself and toward Christ. From various quarters there was, and still is, a tug-of-war—motivated more by nationalism than by Catholicism—over who could claim Mother Teresa as his own. She herself would certainly not have wanted that, though she never denied her roots. One of Mother Teresa's rare statements about herself was: "By birth I am Albanian. I am an Indian citizen. I am a Catholic nun. In what I do, I belong to the whole world, but my heart belongs entirely to Jesus." That makes her position unmistakably clear.

And so, I hope that this book shows Mother Teresa's work and personality in the correct light, and especially how, in everything she did, she always pointed toward Christ. I hope it shows her ultimate aim: to lead everyone to Jesus Christ.

Monsignor Leo Maasburg

1

Love at Second Sight

SHE WAS FASCINATINGLY NORMAL—however extraordinary her life, her effect on people and her ongoing influence, even today. On the one hand, Mother Teresa exceeded all known norms, and, on the other hand, she was completely natural, genuinely "normal"—which was precisely what made her so fascinating. During my time with her and at her side, I observed, studied and admired Mother Teresa. From the very first moment, she reminded me of my grandmother.

In common with my grandmother Mother Teresa had not only hundreds of wrinkles and creases in her face, but also certain generational characteristics. She was strict and disciplined with herself, but at the same time kindly, considerate and extremely patient with others. She also had the thin, severe lips of many older people, which she occasionally, depending on the situation, pushed forward into a pout; she would tilt her head a bit to one side and listen to visitors with a hint of skepticism—and yet with great attentiveness.

At other moments, again with pursed lips, she would move her head back and forth, like a wine connoisseur having his first taste of the new vintage—at such moments, those who knew her sensed that a razor-sharp decision was about to be made. And finally the pursed lips would disappear, often between her wrinkled hands and cheeks; her head would grow heavy and Mother Teresa would support it on her toil-worn hands, clearly marked by arthritis, and, forgetting her surroundings, would linger in conversation with her Lord.

Here we have arrived at an important feature of Mother Teresa's personality: she was herself what she demanded again and again of her Sisters, namely, a "contemplative in the world." All her activities and her attention, which seemed to be directed entirely toward the world, concealed another important part of her nature. The latter—like an iceberg—remained hidden under the surface or, more precisely, was directed inward: contemplative; immersed in meditation on God, His love and His workings in the world. Moreover, she carried within her a personal secret that none of us knew anything about, a profound mystical suffering that became known only after her death: the "dark night of the soul," an unfulfilled and ardent longing for the close presence of God.

On my first visit to Calcutta I was still fairly critical. I wanted to observe in detail in what way Mother Teresa's spirituality and piety affected her activities and those of her Sisters. And so I sat down at a convenient angle from Mother Teresa in the chapel, just to watch how she prayed. She seemed to be totally absorbed while, with profound reverence, she sat kneeling on the floor or on a mat, eyes closed, now and again with her hands pressed into her face.

After a while I discovered that a photographer was nervously pacing up and down outside the chapel door. Evidently he wanted to speak with Mother Teresa but did not dare to go up to her and disturb her. Suddenly a Sister approached him and signaled that he should just approach her. He took off his shoes and went into the chapel, but hesitated to kneel down beside Mother Teresa. Now he will disturb her, I thought—curious as to how she would react.

She must have heard or sensed it when he knelt down beside her on the floor, for she looked up and welcomed him with a radiant smile. Her attention now belonged entirely to the photographer. He presented his business in a few words. She gave him an answer. He stood up and left the chapel. Before he was even outside, Mother Teresa was already completely and utterly immersed again in prayer.

What moved me so much about this short scene was that Mother Teresa gave not even the slightest indication of displeasure or annoyance. On the contrary, it was as though the photographer had brought her a present by disturbing her at prayer. Only later did I understand that Jesus Himself was so present for Mother Teresa in the people whom she met that she—coming out of prayer, and thus out of a lively conversation with Jesus—simply shifted from Jesus to Jesus.

One of the truest and most beautiful ways in which Mother Teresa described herself was something that she once said to a group of journalists. One of the reporters said, "Mother Teresa, what you do is so wonderful!" And she replied, "You know, I am only a little pencil in the hand of God, a God who is about to write a love letter to the world."

Mother Teresa meant that we should allow ourselves to be used by God as we ourselves use a pencil: Just as I need a pencil to write with, so that I can put on paper what I think and want to say, so in a similar way God uses a human being to express what He thinks and wants to say. God is great and yet humble; He uses us imperfect human beings in order to manifest His greatness. If we truly want to belong to Him and serve Him, then we must allow Him to use us in the manner in which He wants to be proclaimed.

But with that I am already anticipating much more of the conclusion than I ought to at the start of this book. So let us begin once again from the beginning.

ço

I had the privilege of meeting Mother Teresa while I was still a student. At that time I was working closely with the exiled Slovak bishop Pavol Hnilica, who lived in Rome and supported the underground Church in the former Eastern Bloc through the charitable organization Pro Fratribus, which he had founded. He had become acquainted with Mother Teresa in 1964 at the Eucharistic Congress in Bombay (today Mumbai) and probably realized immediately what kind of person she was. So he urged Pope Paul VI to invite her to come to Rome and finally succeeded. Bishop Hnilica also helped to establish the first foundation, or house, of Mother Teresa's Sisters in the suburb of Tor Fiscale in Rome.

Since I was working with the Bishop, I was present when Mother Teresa came for a visit, and also when Bishop Hnilica visited her at her foundation, San Gregorio, in Rome, but I preferred to stay in the background. At that time I was inclined to think that I should leave her in peace, especially since on those occasions Mother Teresa was besieged by the great numbers of Czech and Slovak visitors who always surrounded Bishop Hnilica.

Rome, of course, was full of interesting celebrities. I unconsciously placed Mother Teresa in that category as well. But at my very first real encounter with her, she dissolved all my prejudices. Instead of sitting down with the Bishop and her other visitors and doing all the talking, she brought everybody into the chapel, knelt down and remained praying before the Most Blessed Sacrament. She did not want to lead us to herself and to her work, but rather to the Blessed Sacrament!

Ultimately I owe the grace of becoming close to Mother Teresa after I was ordained a priest in 1982, as well as the privilege of accompanying her time and again on her travels over the course of several years, to the fact that Bishop Hnilica had the charism of speaking no English. They were able to understand each other directly if need be, he in Slovak and she in Croatian (both Slavic languages), but when there was a more complicated or detailed matter to discuss, they needed an interpreter. That's where I came in, translating between Mother Teresa's English and Bishop Hnilica's Italian or German.

Once, during one of my first interpreting stints after my ordination, Bishop Hnilica went out and I remained alone with Mother Teresa. I asked her what a newly ordained priest should do if he felt in his heart that he should go to Russia as a missionary. Her answer came as though shot from a pistol: "He should do what his bishop tells him."

I felt as though she was looking clear through me, and so, to justify myself, I asked, "But if the bishop doesn't say anything, what should he do then?"

Mother Teresa reflected briefly and replied, "Then he should do what the Pope tells him."

And that is exactly what happened later: It was indirectly through Pope John Paul II that I eventually traveled with Mother Teresa, first to Moscow and then to Armenia. The secretary of state, Cardinal Angelo Sodano, acting in the Pope's name, gave me the necessary mandate as required by canon law.

೧৲

Pragmatic and very practical by nature, Mother Teresa had a knack for obtaining assistance and support for her work and her plans through chance meetings—of which there were a countless number. So, on my first lengthy encounter with Mother Teresa, once my service as an interpreter for her and my bishop was completed, not a minute passed before she found out that I owned a car. She immediately asked me to take three of her Sisters to the airport that afternoon. And so I found myself that Sunday, at three in the afternoon, in the parking lot in front of San Gregorio, the Sisters' house in Rome. Mother Teresa was already standing there and "handed over" her three Sisters to me. Each one carried an open box on her arm. While loading the trunk I saw the contents of these boxes: a rolled-up sleeping mat, two folded saris, a Bible, a prayer book and a few small personal items.

"Are we taking a trip to the countryside?" I asked the Sisters somewhat teasingly, gesturing toward their light baggage.

"No, to the airport," was their answer.

"And what is your destination?" I wanted to know.

"Argentina," said one beaming Sister, whom I could easily have taken for a teenager.

"And for how long? A week or two?"

"Oh, no; surely for at least five to ten years!"

Still seeking an explanation for their rather meager baggage, I asked when they had learned about this emigration.

"This morning. After the ceremony of our vows, Mother Teresa gave us our new mission! We are so happy!"

In the silence that followed I could only compare my priestly obedience with theirs—the result occupies my thoughts to this day.

I learned that obedience for consecrated religious extends much, much further than it does for secular priests. The Sisters' total availability for the task they are given by their superior has shaped my thinking. Mother Teresa knew exactly what authority is really due to anyone; she was quite definitely not submissive, but she was very obedient. Never would she have undertaken something in order to make a good impression on her superior, or on a bishop or a cardinal. Moreover she could always distinguish precisely between a command given by a bishop that was within his competence and one outside his competence.

Once, when Mother Teresa met Cardinal Franz König unexpectedly at a Synod of Bishops and he asked her how she felt among so many bishops, she answered, "You know, Your Eminence, of course I don't understand everything that they say and report here, but I think that it's perhaps sometimes more important to pray for the bishops than to listen to them."

Although the young Sisters whom I had taken to the airport had received their assignments that same morning, and only then had they learned where they were to travel, they obeyed cheerfully. Later, I often witnessed this kind of send-off, which is part of the symbolic way in which the Missionaries of Charity, in a very poignant way, demonstrate the nature of their vows of poverty, chastity, obedience and "full hearted and free service to the poorest of the poor." After the liturgical ceremony during which the new Sisters took their vows, they would each place a written copy in Mother Teresa's hands. Then they would go into the sacristy, where Mother Teresa would hand each one of them her assignment. The slip of paper would read: "Dear Sister _____,

I am sending you to _____." Mother Teresa would fill in each Sister's name and the appropriate country by hand. At the bottom of each slip of paper she would write: "God bless you. Mother M. Teresa, MC."

I did not yet know all this when I drove the three Sisters to the airport in Rome. Yet I had already sensed something of Mother Teresa's spirit and of her work. When I got back, I wanted to report to her that her Sisters had left safely. Tea and a few cookies were already waiting for me. And then she herself came to thank me, or so I first thought. But instead I already had my next assignment: "Father, could you drive me to the Vatican tomorrow?"

2

In the Vatican

Punctually at half past five the next morning I arrived at
San Gregorio to pick up Mother Teresa. She and a Sister
who was fortunate enough to accompany her on her visit to
the Holy Father were already waiting for their ride. When the
Vatican opened its gates at six, my green Opel with its Munich
license plate was the first car waiting. The Swiss guard waved
us through with a smart salute, and we drove up the ramp
to the Cortile San Damaso (St. Damasus' Courtyard); from
there the Pope's guests take an elevator to the third floor,
where the entrance to the Holy Father's chambers is located.

As I stopped the car in front of the entrance to the elevator,
another Swiss guard saluted. "Good morning, Mother Teresa.
You're much too early. Please wait here." His command was
succinct. So I had the good fortune to wait in the car with
Mother Teresa for almost an hour. That was more than I
had ever hoped for, and I believe that I have never enjoyed
waiting as much as on that occasion.

Mother Teresa sat in the passenger seat, and together we
prayed the fifteen decades of the Rosary and a Quick Novena.
This Quick Novena was, so to speak, Mother Teresa's spiritual
rapid-fire weapon. It consisted of ten Memorares—not nine,
as you might expect from the word "novena." Novenas lasting

nine days were quite common among the congregation of the Missionaries of Charity. But given the host of problems that were brought to Mother Teresa's attention, not to mention the pace at which she traveled, it was often just not possible to allow nine days for an answer from Celestial Management. And so she invented the Quick Novena.

Here are the words of the Memorare:

> Remember, O most gracious Virgin Mary, that never was it known that anyone who fled to your protection, implored your help, or sought your intercession was left unaided. Inspired with this confidence, I fly unto you, O Virgin of virgins, my Mother. To you I come, before you I stand, sinful and sorrowful. O Mother of the Word incarnate, despise not my petitions, but in your clemency hear and answer me. Amen.

Mother Teresa used this prayer constantly: for petitions for the cure of a sick child, before important discussions or when passports went missing, to request heavenly aid when the fuel supply was running short on a nighttime mission and the destination was still far away in the darkness. The Quick Novena had one thing in common with nine-day and even nine-month novenas: confident pleading for heavenly assistance, as the apostles did for nine days in the upper room "together with the women and Mary the mother of Jesus" (Acts 1:14) while waiting for the promised help from the Holy Spirit.

The reason why Mother Teresa always prayed ten Memorares, though, is that she took the collaboration of heaven so much for granted that she always added a tenth Memorare immediately, in thanksgiving for the favor received. So it was on this occasion. We prayed the entire

Rosary while we were waiting in the car. No sooner had we finished the Quick Novena than the Swiss guardsman knocked on the steamed-up windshield and said, "Mother Teresa, it's time!" Mother Teresa and the Sister got out. To keep the guardsman from chasing me out of the beautiful courtyard, I called after Mother Teresa, "Mother, I'll wait here for you until you come back down. Then I'll take you home." But it was to be otherwise.

For she turned around and called, "Quick, Father, you come with us!" Was it the Quick Novena that finally brought about this "Quick, Father. . ."? I had no time to reflect, for Mother Teresa was already on her way to the elevator; she swept aside the timid protest of the Swiss guardsman with a charming "Father is with us!" and a grateful twinkle of her eyes.

I thought I knew why the guardsman let me go along with no further objections. The rules were unequivocal—only those who were on the list of announced guests could enter. And only the names of Mother Teresa and one other Sister were on that list. So it was probably just as clear to the guardsman as it was to me that I had no chance. Even in the company of a saint I would not get past the elevator attendant—much less the civil police in front of the entrance to the Holy Father's apartment.

Mother assured the hesitant elevator attendant no less charmingly, but at the same time quite decisively. "We can start now. Father is with us." Rather than contradict such a clear instruction from Mother Teresa, the elevator attendant obviously preferred to leave it to the civil police to put an end to my intrusion into the papal chambers. As we got out of the elevator it seemed as though that was what he was thinking as he waved to the policeman.

I had already tried again and again to explain to Mother Teresa in the elevator that it is not only unusual but absolutely impossible to make your way into the Pope's quarters unannounced. But even my resistance was useless. She repeated, "No, Father, you are with us." Well, since I could not sink into the floor, there was nothing left for me to do but prepare myself for the final "Out!" just before we reached the desired destination. In my mind I could already hear the elevator attendant and the guardsman whispering, "We told you so," when I crawled back to the car. Would they at least let me wait in the courtyard?

There is a long corridor on the third floor of the Palazzo Apostolico, leading from the elevator to the first great reception hall of the papal apartments—not long enough, however, to convince Mother Teresa that it would be better for me to turn around immediately. "I wouldn't mind at all," I tried to explain timidly.

"You come with us!" she replied firmly. So nothing could be done. Some people called this holy woman a "benevolent dictator"—and I was slowly beginning to understand why.

The walls of the corridor that we were now walking along in silence were lined with splendid paintings and studded with ornamentation. The view out of the large windows was simply breathtaking: At our feet, in the light morning mist, lay the Cortile San Damaso, St. Peter's Square, the Gianicolo Hill with the Pontifical Urbaniana University and the North American College, and, finally, a seemingly endless ocean of roofs: the Eternal City. I had little time, however, to absorb these impressions. Mother Teresa, the Sister and I were coming closer and closer to the door to the papal apartments. In front of it stood two tall policemen in civilian clothes—would this be the definite end of my morning excursion to see the Pope? I was sure of it.

The expected "Out!" was finally delivered in a very friendly and professional tone. The older of the two policemen courteously greeted the foundress of a religious order: "Mother Teresa, good morning! Please come this way. The padre is not announced. He cannot come in." He stepped aside for Mother Teresa, whereas I had stopped walking. She gestured to me, however, that I should keep going, and explained to the policeman, "Father is with us."

But this time even the supernatural charm of a holy woman did not prevail over a Vatican security official who was faithfully following orders. The papal policeman now stepped into Mother Teresa's path and repeated his instruction kindly but definitely, so that there could be no remaining doubt as to who set the rules in this part of the palace: "Mother, your padre has no permission; therefore he cannot come with you!" Given such courteous, yet unassailable, authority, it was quite clear to me what my next step was: make my retreat now and as quickly as possible!

In such situations the difference between success and failure becomes clear: To Mother Teresa the solution to this problem appeared altogether different from the way it appeared to me. She stood there calmly and asked the policeman in a patient tone of voice, "And who can give the priest permission?"

The good man was obviously not prepared for this question. With a helpless shrug of his shoulder he said, "Well, maybe the Pope himself. Or Monsignor Dziwisz. . ."

"Good, then wait here!" was the prompt reply. And Mother Teresa was already weaseling her way beneath the shrugged shoulders of the policeman and heading for the papal chambers. "I will go and ask the Holy Father!"

The poor policeman! After all, one of his most important duties was to safeguard the peace and tranquility of the Pope. And now—it was quite clear to him—this little nun was going to burst into the chapel, snatch the Pope away from his deep prayer, and bother him with a request to admit a simple priest. No, that must not happen! And it was up to him to prevent it!

"*Per amor di Dio*, Mother Teresa!"

A short pause, then Italian-Vatican common sense prevailed and Mother Teresa had won: "Then the padre had better just go with you!"

Turning to me, he said, "Go. Go now!"

An order is an order, and so the "benevolent dictator," for whom I had ever greater esteem, the Sister and I went past the policeman and into the Holy Father's reception hall.

From a door on the opposite side of the hall, a figure approached us: Monsignor Stanisiaw Dziwisz, the Pope's private secretary, who today is a cardinal and the archbishop of Krakow. Shaking Mother Teresa's hand warmly, he looked inquisitively at the padre who so unexpectedly enlarged the group. Mother Teresa saw no need at all to give him an explanation. Instead, her words of greeting were: "Monsignor, the padre will concelebrate Holy Mass with the Holy Father!" She did not ask, "Could he?" or, "Would it be possible?" No, she said, "The padre will. . . !" Clearly Monsignor Dziwisz already knew the "benevolent dictator" better than I did. After examining me with a brief critical glance, he smiled, took my hand and led me into the sacristy, where he explained to me the customs of the house for concelebrating morning Mass with Pope John Paul II. He laughed heartily at the way in which I had intruded into the papal chambers.

With a short bow the Pope acknowledged the presence of Mother Teresa and the Sister in the chapel. Besides them there were only two Polish Sisters from his household. In the sacristy the Holy Father put on his vestments while softly murmuring prayers in Latin.

That Holy Mass was an overwhelming experience and left me with an unexpectedly profound impression. The intense devotion of those two blessed personages of the Universal Church in the silence of the morning and high over the roofs of Rome—it was simply thrilling! It was so intense that I felt as though I was inhaling an atmosphere of peace and love.

3

How to Order a Saint

THE FOLLOWING YEAR—again at a morning Mass in the Pope's private chapel, although this time I was announced—I witnessed the reverence and deep respect that Mother Teresa and Pope John Paul II had for each other, those two great leaders of the Church whom we now also regard as important historical figures. Even the way in which they greeted each other reflected their individual styles: Mother Teresa folded her hands on her breast; John Paul II put his arm around her affectionately. It struck me on that occasion—as it did again and again later on—that they exchanged only a few words. They came directly to the point rather than chatting about things that were not directly connected with the business at hand. As with people who are very close with one another, there was no irrelevant small talk and no unnecessary etiquette.

As soon as they had greeted each other warmly, Mother Teresa came to the point: "Holy Father, we need a saint for our lepers!" When the Pope asked whom Mother Teresa had in mind for this "job," she mentioned Father Damian de Veuster, a Belgian missionary born in 1840 who lived on the Hawaiian Islands among the lepers and cared for the sick until finally he himself died of the disease. Jef, as he was called in the world, was the seventh child of a peasant family and worked on his parents' farm until he entered the Order of the Sacred Hearts of Jesus and Mary in Louvain at the age of twenty and took the religious name Damian (in French, Damien). In 1874 he had himself taken to the island of Moloka'i so that he could look after the lepers who were forced to live there in complete isolation and without any medical care. In 1885 he himself was diagnosed with leprosy. He died in 1889.

"Do you know him, Holy Father?" asked Mother Teresa.

The Pope nodded, and Mother Teresa thought that she had already achieved her aim: "Well then, why wait? When will you declare him a saint?"

But there was a major problem to resolve before they could schedule a canonization: Father Damian had not yet worked certified miracles, and these are required by canon law for a beatification or a canonization.

However, the Holy Father already knew Mother Teresa far too well to get into a lengthy discussion with her. Instead, he instructed her to discuss the matter personally with Cardinal Pietro Palazzini, the prefect of the Congregation for the Causes of Saints. Mother Teresa did not need to be asked twice.

Cardinal Palazzini himself was even quicker; the Holy Father had obviously informed him. The very next day, at a quarter after six in the morning, Cardinal Palazzini knocked on the doors of San Gregorio, the Motherhouse of the Missionaries of Charity, where Mother Teresa lived while she was in Rome. Cardinal Palazzini was very thin and just as short as Mother Teresa. His eyes revealed a sense of humor and a lively intelligence. He was known in the Vatican—and sometimes also feared—for his outstanding theological learning and his special knowledge of canon law. He had been the prefect of the Congregation for the Causes of the Saints for years and was certainly a distinguished adviser to the Pope.

"Mother Teresa, the Holy Father has sent me to you. What can I do for you?" was the first thing he said, which I translated for him.

"Your Eminence, we need a saint for our lepers," Mother Teresa repeated her request for a new saint.

"And who might that be?" the Cardinal wanted to know.

"Father Damian de Veuster. Do you know him?"

"Yes, Mother Teresa. But as you know, there is a minor difficulty: he hasn't worked a miracle yet, and we need that for his canonization."

"That may be so," replied Mother Teresa, "but in Holy Scripture it says. . . ," and then she held a Bible, open at chapter 15, verse 13 of Saint John's Gospel, in front of the eyes of the startled Cardinal and read, " 'Greater love has no man than this, that a man lay down his life for his friends.' And that's exactly what Father Damian did. Isn't he already canonized by the Bible; what are we waiting for?"

She had led off with her strongest argument and was now waiting to receive her "reward." But her plan did not go quite that smoothly.

Cardinal Palazzini took a deep breath and played his trump card: "You're right of course, Mother Teresa. But you know, for over four hundred years we have had a tradition within the Church that three certified miracles are required for a canonization. And Father Damian hasn't even worked one miracle yet!"

"Yes," she replied with great enthusiasm. "This would be a good opportunity to change that tradition!" Another goal! Success seemed within her grasp. "After all, the Bible takes precedence over canon law," she added, to put an end to the discussion.

But the Cardinal gave a smile that was both kindly and clever and said, "Mother Teresa, you're quite right. But don't you think it would be much simpler for you to ask the Good Lord for these miracles than for us to change our four-hundred-year-old tradition?"

That was the only time that I ever saw Mother Teresa speechless and without an answer.

After a while she finally said, "Well, then, let's pray!" The clever Cardinal from Italy had kept the upper hand.

℘

So as not to leave Mother Teresa in the lurch, and to show her that the preparatory work for a canonization is immense and very important and in this case had already been completed years earlier, the Cardinal invited her to visit the archives of the congregation. There he showed her the mountains of documents that had been accumulated for the beatification of Father Damian.

"Which volume is the most important for Father Damian's beatification?" Mother Teresa inquired for the third time, apparently taking a great interest in the hundreds of weighty tomes.

The entire staff of the congregation had gathered when they heard that Mother Teresa was in the building. The Cardinal explained to his unusual guest, patiently and with evident pride, the archive's long rows of books and documents and the complexity of the canonization process.

When Mother Teresa urgently asked yet again which was the most important volume of all for the beatification or canonization of Father Damian, Cardinal Palazzini finally dispatched a staff member. He climbed a ladder and returned with an old and heavy leatherbound tome, covered in decades of dust. When he dropped it heavily onto the large oak table, a cloud of dust arose from it, showing its importance.

"So that is really the most important volume for the canonization of Father Damian?" Mother Teresa wanted to be sure.

"Yes, Mother Teresa, because in this volume. . ."

The Cardinal had just launched into another patient explanation, but had not finished the first sentence, when Mother Teresa reached deep into her blue-gray carrier bag. She brought out a small Miraculous Medal and a piece of sticky tape with which she fastened the medal to the front of the heavy tome. Interrupting the Cardinal's explanation, she said, "So, we've done the most important thing; we can go now!" We left behind a disconcerted cardinal and his staff.

So who "won" in the end? God in His goodness allowed both these great individuals their victory. The miracle that Mother Teresa prayed for happened a short time later. And at the same time, a reorganization of the procedures for beatification reduced the number of miracles required from three to one.

Father Damian de Veuster, the hero of Moloka'i, who himself died of leprosy after four years of great suffering, was beatified by Pope John Paul II on June 4, 1995, with Mother Teresa in attendance. She was overjoyed to have a saint for her lepers who was one of them, and to whom they could turn in their distress with complete confidence. The Belgian missionary was canonized by Pope Benedict XVI on October 11, 2009, in St. Peter's Square in Rome.

෴

It is easy to explain why Mother Teresa attached such great importance to a saint for lepers. From ancient times, lepers have been cut off from society, indeed, even from their closest relatives. Because of the fear of contagion they have had to live as outcasts, far from inhabited areas. Just as Saint Francis of Assisi once embraced a leper, so, too, Mother Teresa wanted to show kindness and tenderness to these poor people, especially since the great majority of lepers live in India. In 1957 she took in her first leper patients. That same year she had her first Sisters trained in the treatment of leprosy. In lepers she saw "especially beloved children of God" who, in their suffering, shared in Christ's Passion.

Mother Teresa soon established mobile medical units for the care and treatment of lepers, but also permanent leprosaria for the most serious cases. The "popemobile" that was used at the Eucharistic Congress in Bombay was subsequently given by Pope Paul VI to Mother Teresa, who auctioned it off and thereby financed an entire leper colony. In 1959 she founded a large center for lepers, and later a village 185 miles from Calcutta, in which lepers are employed in workshops under the direction of the Missionaries of Charity and earn their own living. She called the village Shanti Nagar (Place of Peace).

4

Mother Teresa's Second Vocation

IN ORDER TO UNDERSTAND Mother Teresa's very special devotion to the poorest of the poor, we have to consider her central experience of being called and to begin at the beginning. In 1928 she entered the Loreto Sisters in Dublin in order to go to India as a missionary. In early 1929 she began her novitiate in Darjeeling in northern India. (Darjeeling is a town in West Bengal at the foot of the Himalayas, about sixty-five hundred feet above sea level.) In 1931 she took her temporary vows, and in 1937 her perpetual vows. So she had already been in a religious order for one and a half decades and was striving to live a holy life, with everything that that involved, when on September 10, 1946, while on a train journey to her annual retreat, she had a life-changing experience.

It happened like this: Mother Teresa had set out, once again, on the journey to Darjeeling. While still on the way to the railroad station in Calcutta, she saw countless poor people; large sections of the population had fallen into indescribable misery since the most recent riots. At every station where the overcrowded train stopped, the consequences of the violence were visible: crowds of people living in utter wretchedness.

During the long train ride she heard Jesus' words quite clearly in her heart: "I thirst." She heard them very intensely, and she felt in her heart God's overwhelming love for her. Later she would write, "This is the first time that the thirst of Jesus is being proclaimed." In Saint John's Gospel, these words, "I thirst," are almost the last words that Jesus speaks before His death on the Cross: "After this, Jesus, knowing that all was now finished, said (to fulfill the Scripture), 'I thirst'" (Jn 19:28).

On that train journey to Darjeeling, Mother Teresa realized deep in her heart that God does not just love us in a general way, but that His words "I thirst" are the ultimate and supreme expression of His love, an expression of His longing for the love of His creation and for the salvation of their souls. Jesus spoke these words on the Cross, for the Cross is the "act" by which He tries to convince us of God's love, which is limitless and extends beyond death.

This was the moment when Mother Teresa recognized the true core of her vocation. She used the ten-day retreat in Darjeeling to ponder this insight, and especially to reflect on the message she had received from Jesus. When she returned to Calcutta she was certain that her life was about to change, and how it would change. She was determined to serve Jesus in the poorest of the poor. And she wanted to identify with Him through a life of total poverty. She resolved to live a life of poverty among the poor, to possess nothing, and to trust entirely in God's Providence and guidance.

The decision to leave the Sisters of Loreto after eighteen years was not an easy one for Mother Teresa. Although she recognized this step as the will of Jesus, it was very important to her that she did not take it against the will of the ecclesiastical authorities or without their approval. She turned to the superior of her congregation; she had several long conversations with Ferdinand Périer, the archbishop of Calcutta; and she wrote to her general superior in Dublin to explain the reason for her request—to follow Christ's insistent and repeated invitation.

On April 2, 1948, Pope Pius XII, in response to an application by Archbishop Périer, gave Mother Teresa permission to live as a religious Sister outside the convent, put her under obedience to the Archbishop, and required her to keep the rules of her congregation.

On August 16, 1948, the day after the Feast of the Assumption of the Blessed Virgin Mary, she changed out of the religious habit of the Loreto Sisters and left her convent. The schoolgirls had prepared a farewell song. Carrying a suitcase and a handbag, Mother Teresa walked toward the gate, but stopped in the middle of the many hundreds of students. The girls began to sing, but soon, one after another, they started to sob. After a few minutes they were wailing so much that they had to stop singing. Mother Teresa bent down, picked up her luggage and left—out through the gate and directly into the neighboring slum. She did not look back, but closed the gate of the convent behind her for good, so as to live out her calling to the poorest of the poor.

☙

Out on the streets of Calcutta, it was mainly through the children—she was an excellent teacher—that Mother Teresa gained access to the people living in misery: the homeless, the sick, the infirm, the handicapped, the marginalized. In everything she placed herself completely and utterly at the disposal of Divine Providence. She did not want to develop strategic plans or worry about money matters—from the very beginning she knew it was to be entirely His work. And the Lord rewarded her trust.

One day Mother Teresa gave her last rupee to a priest, not knowing what she herself was going to live on the next day. That evening a stranger knocked at her door and handed her an envelope with fifty rupees, "for your work."

Years later, when the Sisters were already feeding thousands of people in Calcutta, they suddenly ran short of food. They wanted to tell the poor people that there would be nothing for them that weekend, but Mother Teresa stopped them and withdrew to the chapel to pray. The next morning a truck brought great quantities of milk, bread and marmalade. What had happened? The government had closed the schools for some reason, and the food for the schoolchildren's midday meal had been rerouted by some thoughtful person to the Missionaries of Charity.

Another time the flour ran out and there was no money to buy more. The Sister who was assigned to the kitchen went sadly to Mother Teresa, who gave her clear instructions: "You are responsible for the kitchen? Then go to the chapel and pray!" While she was praying, a stranger rang the doorbell and delivered a huge sack of flour.

During their first years in Vienna, the Missionaries of Charity were paying a relatively high rent for the premises they were using for the poor. When I told Mother Teresa my worries about this she just said, "God will take care of it!" We were on our way to see Cardinal Franz König at the time. After the visit, just as we were about to drive off again, two elderly ladies stopped us. Mother Teresa had another appointment scheduled and so it took me some self-control not to put the ladies off to a later date. While I waited, with the motor running, Mother Teresa spoke with them for quite a long time. Later, at the first red traffic light, she opened her patched handbag; in it was a bundle of about 300,000 Austrian schillings (then about $15,000 [U.S.]) that one of the ladies had given her. She then asked, "Do you understand now?"

Mother Teresa and her Sisters had many such stories. They knew that miracles happen every day—or, more precisely, that Jesus will not abandon His work. In the poor and the suffering, Mother Teresa really saw the Body of Christ, her Savior, Whom she served with dedication and without considering any arguments about what was expedient. Not for one moment did she want the Missionaries of Charity to be *her* work; they were to be exclusively *His* work.

This lack of planning for future needs, which was sometimes quite frightening, left room for Providence. In other words, the work was carried out in such a way that it could only succeed if it was completely and entirely His work. And it did succeed—it grew and flourished. When she died, Mother Teresa left behind a religious family that consisted of five congregations in 592 houses all over the globe. Her aim in all this was to show Jesus to the world in the poorest of the poor.

In the congregation of the Missionaries of Charity, not only is the individual member poor, as in many other Catholic religious orders; the whole community is poor. There is no fixed income or accumulation of property. Because the Sisters take a vow freely to serve the poorest of the poor without recompense, they accept no income for the service they give. They work hard and earn nothing—at least not in the material sense. Mother Teresa was always unshakably convinced that God, in His provident love, would give them exactly as much as they needed for their work and when they needed it. He did, and still does today, through donors, benefactors and patrons from all over the world.

Many people found Mother Teresa's trust in God's Providence difficult to understand. She was firmly convinced that His Providence would always supply what was needed. One story in particular helped me understand this. One day the president of an international business came to see Mother Teresa and to offer her a plot of land in Bombay. Before he did so, however, he asked her in a professional tone, "Mother Teresa, how do you manage your budget?"

Mother Teresa answered with a question of her own, "Who sent you here?"

He replied, "I felt prompted from within to come."

Mother Teresa smiled at him. "Other people have come, like you, to see me and told me the same thing. It's clear that God has sent you, and all those others, and you all take care of our material needs. So you, too, were moved by the grace of God. You are my budget."

If the Sisters had not trusted completely and utterly in Divine Providence, they would have had to despair. They were responsible for thousands and thousands of sick and dying people, the hungry, the infirm and little children. Why do we see them smiling all the time? Because they live from and for God's loving care.

5

The Poor Are Wonderful People

IN ORDER TO CORRECTLY UNDERSTAND the importance of Mother Teresa's charism, her extraordinary spiritual gift, we need to bear in mind that her vocation was not directed toward the poor in general, but rather "to the poorest of the poor," those who could not help themselves and had no one to take care of them.

Mother Teresa was certainly not a guru who expected everybody to imitate her; she had a great respect for other vocations. "If you are called to educate young people, then that is your vocation. That is what God wants from you." And I often heard her say this simple sentence: "What you do, I cannot do. What I do, you cannot do. But together we can do something beautiful for God."

Moreover, Mother Teresa saw poverty neither as an ideal in itself nor as a divinely ordained destiny. "God did not create poverty. We created poverty because we do not share with one another."

During my first encounters with Mother Teresa, her openness, her insistence on immediately inviting the poor into a newly opened house—indeed, she almost forced them to come in—struck me as somewhat worrying. Wherever she opened a new house, all the poor people in the neighborhood were invited to the first Holy Mass. Mother Teresa wanted it that way. Looking back, I understand that it was Jesus Whom she wanted to have there, both in the form of the Eucharist and in the poor.

For my part, I have to admit, the people who joined us for the inaugural celebrations were not exactly the kind of people that I had imagined for the first Mass with Mother Teresa in a new place—they would, most of the time, not qualify as churchgoers, they sometimes looked a bit shifty, and often they were not exactly sweet smelling.

An example of this occurred in Vienna. The liturgy at Mass was beautiful; the Sisters had sung wonderfully. After the Mass the Sisters prayed their usual four prayers together with Mother Teresa and then went back to their work, in this case setting up the newly founded house. I came out of the sacristy back into the chapel to say my thanksgiving prayers. The last of the people at the Mass seemed to have gone. I knelt down behind the altar.

Then I noticed a tramp, a homeless man, sitting on the other side of the altar. He had open wounds on his legs. I got the impression that he was slightly tipsy. I did not feel very comfortable about this situation, and I hoped he would go soon.

So I said my prayers piously, though not very attentively, behind the altar. Suddenly the tramp began talking out loud. At first I was frightened: I thought he was talking to me.

But as I listened I realized—with an increasingly guilty conscience—that he was praying.

"Yeah, Jesus, I'm here. Never woulda thought. Dunno if it ruined your day or not, man, but I really, really like it here." He spoke with Jesus like this for at least five minutes, very personally and, I thought, beautifully. It was perhaps the most natural and heartfelt prayer I have ever heard. He clearly had not seen me behind the altar. He thought he was all alone with his Jesus and could speak with Him undisturbed. This man changed my attitude toward street people.

That experience proved to me what Mother Teresa so often said: "The poor are wonderful people." Usually we only see them from the outside, in the "distressing disguise" of poverty, a kind of external skin that we do not find particularly attractive. Only rarely, as on that occasion in Vienna, do we also see their hearts. That is why Mother Teresa often used to say, "Never judge."

☙

The conditions in which the poorest of the poor lived in Calcutta at that time, and still live today, are unimaginable. The air in the city was so polluted that if you went out onto the street in the morning in a clean shirt to buy the *Calcutta Herald Tribune*, you returned with your sleeves and collar all dirty. The heat, the humidity, the dust and dirt stirred up by the passing cars were indescribable. It was especially bad when there was no wind. Then the many, many burning garbage heaps produced smoke that hung over Calcutta as in a bell jar.

Cleaning was therefore part of the Sisters' daily life. They cleaned not only their own house, but also the houses of the poorest of the poor when they went to visit them. They cleaned ceaselessly. When they came home after a "cleaning project," the first thing they had to do was wash their own saris.

Cleaning is life-sustaining. And everything that sustains life comes from the Holy Spirit. So by cleaning we encounter the Holy Spirit in our everyday lives!

If a dying man is not washed, he dies very quickly. Keeping a dying person clean is one of the Sisters' most important and most valuable duties. The House for the Dying is scrubbed thoroughly every day. Everything, I mean everything, is cleaned. The Sisters are engaged in a constant battle against dirt, both physical and spiritual pollution!

For the Missionaries of Charity, the chapel, where the Most Blessed Sacrament is kept, is always the center of every house. The things in it are especially treasured and should, if possible, be beautiful. Of course there are always differences in taste. Mother Teresa, for instance, considered glow-in-the-dark statues of the Mother of God very beautiful. Others, legitimately, had other views. Tasteful or not, the statues were certainly clean.

The large chapel in the Motherhouse, for example, was located on Lower Circular Road in Calcutta, a six-lane road, which at that time was not paved with asphalt. A tram ran down the middle, and cars and trucks drove to the left and right. With every truck that drove by the house, a cloud of dust wafted into the chapel. The noise from the street was so loud that once, when the Archbishop came to celebrate Mass with the Sisters, he insisted on installing a microphone and a loudspeaker. Many of the Sisters wept with emotion because, for the first time in years, they could not only participate in the Mass but could also hear it. They had never understood much of the sermon before because of the noise that welled up from the street. They only knew what the Gospel of the day was about because they read it themselves before Mass.

That, too, was a form of poverty, and Mother Teresa defended it with an iron will. It took an archbishop to insist that a microphone should be installed.

Despite the microphone, every time that I celebrated Mass in that house, one could scarcely understand anything.

The noise of the cars rattling by on Circular Road, and the shouting of the people on the street, were truly unimaginable. I could not resist pointing out to Mother Teresa that it was unreasonable to celebrate Holy Mass there, because the noise was like a waterfall. Her answer was brief: "It's music, Father."

And then there was the dirt. The floor of the chapel was swept three times a day; the altar cloths and carpets were beaten. Each time, a thick layer of dust collected again immediately. In the sacristy, however, things were always sparkling clean, for that was the Sisters' responsibility and an expression of their love for the Eucharist. I was never given an alb that was not freshly washed.

Yet at that time there was only one source of water in the entire Motherhouse. They got up early in the mornings to pump water so that they could wash their saris in strict rotation every day. Since there were three hundred Sisters, this lasted several hours. When I saw the Sisters crowded around the pump by 4:20 in the morning, it was clear that they themselves were truly living like the poorest of the poor, absolutely in keeping with Mother Teresa's saying "We cannot help the poor if we ourselves do not know what poverty is."

Whenever she was in Calcutta, Mother Teresa accompanied the group of volunteer coworkers to the Nirmal Hriday (Pure Heart), the House for the Dying. This house was, so to speak, her favorite child. After morning Mass, before breakfast, she usually gave a short talk and then went with the group to the House for the Dying. I noticed that on these occasions she seemed somewhat agitated and nervous. You could tell that she was anxious to get on with things. As soon as the groups were ready, she would lead them quickly to the House for the Dying. Once there, she would personally give each new volunteer his assignment. She would take each volunteer by the hand, one at a time, and lead him through the rows of sick and dying people, lay the volunteer's hand on one person's forehead, and tell him exactly what to do next: Give the dying person something to eat, or just sit by him, pray beside him, or shave him. That was very helpful; being with a dying person is not easy, especially for young Europeans or Americans who have never seen someone die.

Finally, when each volunteer had his assignment and was carrying it out, she would position herself on the slightly raised doorstep at the entrance, from which she could oversee everything. Then she would smile broadly and contentedly. One could see it clearly—because of her firm belief in the presence of Christ in the poorest of the poor, she was only relaxed and happy when she had put the volunteers physically in touch with the dying.

When Pope John Paul II came to Calcutta, she did exactly the same with him: She took him by the hand, led him to a dying person and said, "Holy Father, please bless him."

Her job was not to convert people, for only God does that. Her job was "to put you in touch with Jesus." By personally leading the volunteers and even the Pope to a dying person, she connected them to Jesus!

For we encounter Jesus—and this was Mother Teresa's deepest conviction—first in the Most Blessed Sacrament and second in the poorest of the poor, indeed, in every fellow human being who is suffering. For her, the presence of Jesus in the poorest of the poor was just as real as in the Eucharist. Jesus teaches, "Truly, I say to you, as you did it to one of the least of these my brethren, you did it to me" (Mt 25:40).

Mother Teresa sometimes held up the five fingers of one hand to explain this. The whole Gospel, she said, could be counted on five fingers: "You-did-it-to-me!"

An American journalist who observed Mother Teresa attending to a sick man with foul-smelling ulcers is supposed to have said in disgust that he would never do that for a million dollars. And she replied, "Yes, for a million dollars I wouldn't do it either." She did it for Jesus.

☙

We may rightly assume that Jesus' "thirst" on the Cross does not only express a physical need but also has a deeper spiritual dimension. He says, "I thirst," and takes the vinegar that they offer Him—whereas He refused the drugged wine at the beginning of the Crucifixion. After all the torments and tortures, at three in the afternoon in the midday heat of Jerusalem, they give Jesus vinegar instead of water. His lips were probably cracked and bleeding. The vinegar caused unimaginable pain.

But its spiritual significance is even deeper: Jesus began His public ministry by turning water into very good wine at the wedding feast of Cana. And at the end of His public ministry the soldiers offered him vinegar—wine that had gone bad.

The vinegar was there beside the Cross because, after a crucifixion, the Roman soldiers washed their hands and arms in it. It was a kind of soap. This vinegar was the dregs of the dirt—yet Jesus took it as a gift for His thirst. Applied to us, this means that God's love takes even the vinegar of our life and accepts it. The vinegar stands for all our sins, our negligence, our weaknesses, our failures and our betrayals—the dregs of our life.

This explanation by Father Joseph Langford, the co-founder of the Missionaries of Charity Fathers, helps us to grasp Mother Teresa's understanding of Jesus' words on the Cross: God yearns so much for us that we can entrust ourselves completely to Him, again and again. The world will always try to draw us away from this "belonging to God." The world wants us to belong to it, and we are in fact fairly firmly rooted in it.

This message of Jesus on the Cross, "I thirst," becomes the key word for understanding Mother Teresa's whole work. It is a message that attempts to remind us of what Jesus yearns for: love for Him and love for souls, that is, for our fellow human beings.

A common gesture that we use in our culture to express love for someone is an embrace, a hug. In order to hug somebody, I have to open my arms. A boxer's stance makes an embrace impossible. It symbolizes the opposite of love: defensiveness, preventative aggression, mistrust, violence. Jesus on the Cross spreads His arms out to embrace us all, to embrace mankind.

Mother Teresa had the gift of putting complicated theological concepts into very simple short sentences and slogans that were easy to remember. Her dedication to Jesus in the poorest of the poor is best explained by an image from Calcutta. Early one morning we saw hundreds, indeed thousands, of people who had spent the night on the street and were lying there in long rows. Mother Teresa said, "Look, Father; there's Jesus, waiting to be loved."

Once, as we were approaching Shanti Nagar station after a train journey of several hours, I began to feel uncomfortable. How would I react to a whole village of lepers? I told Mother Teresa that I was a little nervous about visiting the leprosarium.

I was feeling uneasy and anxious. She replied, "Father, you will meet Jesus there in His distressing disguise as the poorest of the poor. Our visit will bring joy, for the most terrible poverty is loneliness and the feeling of being unloved. The worst disease today is not leprosy or tuberculosis, but the feeling of being unwanted." Her words reminded me of something else that she had said: "There is more hunger in the world for love and appreciation than for bread."

As we went through the leprosarium with Mother Teresa, a woman in an advanced stage of the disease began singing in a beautiful voice. She was singing to thank Mother Teresa for all the care and love that she and her fellow sufferers received there. I was very moved and began to understand why the deep longing for love can only be satisfied when people are filled with God—not just with money and bread.

Sometimes Mother Teresa was accused of not "helping people to help themselves." Metaphorically speaking, she was reproached for giving poor people a fish, rather than giving them a fishing rod and teaching them how to fish. Mother Teresa's answer was: "My poor people are too weak to hold the fishing rod themselves." Then, with a twinkle in her eye, she added, "But if they are ever well enough to hold a fishing rod, then our critics can go ahead and teach them how to fish!"

Once, when we were discussing whether it was right to give all that help without any recompense, Mother Teresa said, "Many people say, 'Mother Teresa, you are spoiling the poor, because you give everything free of charge.' But no one spoils us as much as God Himself. Look, you have good eyes and can read. What if God were to demand money from you because He gave you your eyes? Or look at how the sun is shining outside. What if God were to tell us, 'You must work five hours to get two hours of sunlight'? I once told a religious Sister: 'There are many congregations that spoil the rich, and so surely it will not hurt if one congregation spoils the poor.'"

6

Mother Teresa's Business

ONCE, ON A STOPOVER between flights, we spent the night at the Missionaries of Charity Sisters' house in Miami. A man was sitting in front of the house in a car, waiting. I spoke to him and he told me the following story. He was not a member of a church; he was an architect by profession. His wife had gotten to know the Missionaries of Charity just after they arrived in Miami. She was a good-hearted person and helped them in the soup kitchen, with the poor, and wherever she was needed. He put up with this and used to pick his wife up there after work. One day he drove up and was waiting for his wife in the car—just as he was doing on the day when he told me this story.

His wife came out of the soup kitchen accompanied by a small, elderly Sister and introduced Mother Teresa to him. Mother Teresa thanked him profusely for allowing and enabling his wife to volunteer with the Sisters. Then she asked him what he did for a living.

"I'm an architect."

"Oh, wonderful; then I'm sure you can make a few photocopies for me."

"I'd be delighted to. What should I copy?"

Mother Teresa rummaged around and brought out a little business card. It read:

>*The fruit of silence is prayer.*
>*The fruit of prayer is faith.*
>*The fruit of faith is love.*
>*The fruit of love is service.*
>*The fruit of service is peace.*

She read the text aloud to him very slowly. "Could you make a few photocopies of this?"

"Yes, very good; I'd be happy to. How many do you need? Ten? Twenty?"

"Thirty thousand, please."

When I asked him whether he had done it, he laughed: "Yes, indeed. I've made a lot of copies. And I've also built two houses for Mother Teresa since then, a nursing home and a house for the Sisters."

Mother Teresa's request for a few copies had developed into a lifelong friendship. And, incidentally, the friendly, helpful architect had also found his way back to the Faith.

Mother Teresa's "business card," which is certainly unique, was inspired by a very well-to-do Indian businessman, a Hindu who wanted to give a gift to the Sisters. So that Mother Teresa might know who he was and what business he was in, he handed her his business card. She looked at it for a long time and then said, "That's a wonderful idea!"

Some of the people watching may have thought that she wanted to get into the same business as him. "What's a good idea?" the Sisters asked.

"We need a business card too!" exclaimed Mother Teresa.

And that is how the visiting card with the text quoted above came into being. On the back of the card Mother Teresa added, "Mary, mother of Jesus, be mother to me now."

That was her "business card." Her own name did not appear anywhere on it—just her business.

The Kolping family in northern Germany once handed Mother Teresa a generous check toward her work. As so often on these occasions, there was a big buffet. Mother Teresa never asked for such receptions; rather, she put up with them. During the buffet, someone sitting across from her commented indignantly that it was scandalous that all the food left over after the buffet would have to be thrown away. Mother Teresa was very shocked and asked why. They explained to her that that was the law, because of health regulations. This immediately became a real matter of concern for her. Although she could not change the law, she made a lot of people think about it.

After the reception she went to her next appointment in a helicopter that the German chancellor Helmut Kohl had placed at her disposal. Then, as if by magic, she produced rolls, sandwiches, fruit and pastries from her bag. When we asked, astonished, where she had gotten all these wonderful gifts, she just said, "It's obvious. The reception was given for me, so I took as much with me as I could."

One of the airlines that Mother Teresa used very often was Pan Am. The staff were very friendly toward her. Whether she had an economy ticket or had not even booked yet, she was always put in first class as a matter of principle. She was often given VIP treatment at airports—she would be met by stewardesses as she left the plane and taken directly to the VIP lounge. The stewardesses took care of her luggage and dealt with the passport formalities. Meanwhile, she was able to rest in the lounge. Mother Teresa's entourage also got this special treatment—a luxury to which we unfortunately became accustomed rather quickly.

At first, I was surprised that Mother Teresa did not mind this special treatment from the airline—or refuse it. On the contrary, we got the impression that she accepted it without objection. But when we were with some other airline and this special treatment was not possible, or the staff did not know who Mother Teresa was, I was always rather disappointed, whilst she did not even seem to notice.

On the very first flight on which I had the privilege of accompanying Mother Teresa, I was not at all sure what my duties involved. Several fellow passengers came to me and asked whether they might speak with Mother Teresa for a moment. One stewardess asked, "Father, do you think I might speak to Mother Teresa? This is the fourth time that I have had the joy of accompanying her on a flight."

I said, "This is my first trip with Mother Teresa. So you know her much better than I do." A few minutes later the stewardess was close to tears as Mother Teresa inquired whether her daughter had found a job yet and then gave her a Miraculous Medal to keep for herself and one for her daughter. But Mother Teresa also had a request: "Please don't forget to give us everything that's left over when we get off, for our poorest of the poor." At least eight neatly packed bags, filled with sandwiches and chocolates, were brought to the VIP lounge afterward and given to Mother Teresa for the poor. The stewardess had not even forgotten the plastic cutlery.

During the flight the stewardess must have told the captain that Mother Teresa was sitting in first class, because the co-pilot came out to greet her. But since she was asleep, he walked noiselessly past her, took off his cap and announced to the passengers that Mother Teresa was on the flight. Anyone who wanted to make a donation for her poor people could give it to him now. He went once through the whole airplane, and when he came back to the front he had more than six hundred U.S. dollars in his cap.

Yes, the Lord gives to His own even whilst they are asleep!

When one of her Sisters handed her the rather large sum of money that had been collected while she was taking her nap, Mother Teresa said contentedly, "Sister, I think I should do that more often." Later I saw this again and again: fellow passengers very quietly placing a donation on her seat or taking a collection while she slept.

Usually though, she slept little on flights. Instead, she prayed her Breviary first—the regular Liturgy of the Hours of the Catholic Church—and then the Rosary. When she had finished praying, she would take a whole sheaf of papers out of her bag, put them in front of her on the folding table, and simply continue writing where she had left off the last time. She frequently nodded off because she was often very short of sleep or exhausted from jet lag. But as soon as she awoke, she would continue writing where she had left off.

So far, more than five thousand letters that she wrote to various groups of people have emerged: to children, politicians, families, religious orders. There was no idling time in the discipline that she imposed on herself. She would never waste time; while her traveling companions were sleeping or reading, she was always working and offering people comfort and advice in her letters.

That too was part of Mother Teresa's "business."

Once we were driving through what was then still Soviet Moscow. As we hurried along the street from one engagement to the next, we suddenly realized that there were no happy faces to be seen—only sad, preoccupied and anxious faces. We pointed this out to Mother Teresa and she replied, "Yes, here it's very easy to understand that every time we smile at someone it's an act of love. It's a gift for that person, something very beautiful."

✿

Her Sisters' house in Zagreb was still fairly new. Mother Teresa decided to stop over to visit them on the way back from a visit to Munich to make sure that everything was all right. Tito's Yugoslavia had not yet crumbled, and the Communist regime, with all its checkpoints, food shortages and bureaucratic chicanery, was still firmly in the saddle.

As so often happened, the next stage of our trip was not yet definitely planned. We were most probably going to Warsaw next. So on the morning of our departure, I went from Kaptol Hill—on which the Sisters' house in Zagreb was located at that time—down into the old city to a travel agency to buy two plane tickets to Warsaw, for Mother Teresa and myself. Patience was not exactly one of my virtues, and it took a lot of self-control for me to wait in line for an hour and a half until, at about ten o'clock, I finally got the tickets.

No sooner was I back on Kaptol Hill than Mother Teresa called me and said, "Father, I'm very sorry, but we're not going to Warsaw. We have to go back to Munich. Could you please see whether you can still exchange the tickets?" So I went back down into the city and waited again in a long line for forty minutes. I finally managed to book the tickets just before lunch. I appeared again at the Sisters' house, where they were already at their midday prayers, with the two tickets for Munich.

As they were coming out of the chapel after prayers, I met the Sister Superior and murmured, "This chaotic planning is really terrible!"

She smiled back. "Father, don't you know what the abbreviation MC after our name really stands for?"

"No. What?"

She enlightened me: "Not just 'Missionary of Charity' but also 'Much Confusion!'"

My spiritual equilibrium had been somewhat restored by her humor when Mother Teresa came past and said, "Father, I'm really very sorry but we have to go to Warsaw after all! We can still change the tickets, can't we?"

Yet again I had to go down into the city center, wait in line, beg, and swallow their sarcastic comments. As if by a miracle, I was back at three in the afternoon, just in time to drive to the airport. The plane was supposed to leave shortly after five o'clock. I was quite proud to have rebooked our flights without losing any money, but at the same time rather unnerved by the "much confusion."

When I was at last sitting beside Mother Teresa on the airplane, I could not help a slightly snide comment. "Mother Teresa, I learned today what the abbreviation MC really means: not 'Missionary of Charity' but 'Much Confusion.'"

With an indescribably charming smile Mother Teresa turned to me and said, "But, Father, do you know what else it means? It also means: More Confusion, Mental Case, Multiple Change..."

She gave several other meanings that I no longer remember. With a twinkle of her eye she had managed to melt all my anger at the poor organization and planning.

7

Tell Them about Jesus!

ONE OF THE HOUSES of the Missionaries of Charity in Vienna had just been founded when Mother Teresa came to me one evening and asked whether I would give a retreat for the Sisters there. I was a newly ordained priest at the time, and this was naturally a great honor. I was well aware that Mother Teresa was very careful in selecting priests to give retreats for her Sisters. It was always very important to her that the Sisters should receive a simple but solid Catholic formation, and also that they should have the opportunity to strengthen and deepen it.

Very conscious of the honor, I said with some embarrassment, "Gladly. When should we start?"

"Tomorrow," she answered.

She had caught me by surprise. I had never given a retreat before. "Mother, what should I talk about?" I pleaded in dismay.

"Talk about Jesus. What else?"

As time went on, I noticed that she always said this to priests: They should simply talk about Jesus, in other words, describe how they themselves have experienced Jesus in faith.

But now that I had to give four forty-five-minute talks a day, what precisely should I say? I did not know. But then I reflected: If Mother Teresa gives me an assignment like this,

55

the Holy Spirit will surely help. I began to browse through books, read the Spiritual Exercises of Saint Ignatius at record speed, and then, that same evening, the Holy Spirit slipped a series of audio cassettes by Father Hans Buob about the Mass into my hands. I was up until three in the morning copying excerpts from the cassettes and translating them into English.

The next day, using these notes, I gave my talks, divided into four sections and illustrated with my own stories as they occurred to me.

So it went on each day. In the evenings I hurried home, sat down immediately at the tape recorder and wrote out excerpts from the next cassette. Eight cassettes for an eight-day retreat; the Sisters' spiritual exercises always last exactly eight days! Even today I meet Sisters from that retreat who tell me that they can clearly remember my presentations. No doubt that this was the work of the Holy Spirit, making use of Father Buob and of me.

Mother Teresa herself attended for the first few hours, then she had to leave because she had other duties; but I think she wanted to keep an eye on this beginner. She was always concerned and wanted to know what priests were teaching her Sisters.

I had the privilege of giving retreats for Mother Teresa's Sisters on many other occasions. Once I asked a regional superior whether there was a topic that was important to her Sisters that I should mention. To my surprise she answered, "How to deal with crazy priests." Clearly that was an important challenge in the life of the Sisters: getting along with all kinds of priests, from those who invented their own Eucharistic Prayers to those who had all sorts of problems in their personal lives.

Many priests enjoyed the fact that Mother Teresa always treated them with great respect and paid special attention to them—compared with the attention she paid to the volunteers or even to her Sisters. At mealtimes, when arranging seating, during periods of rest, and when considering their comfort, she always looked after priests like a mother. But why did she love priests so much?

I suspect that one major reason was contained in the answer that Mother Teresa gave to a journalist who asked the secret of her worldwide success: "Every day, every morning, I receive Holy Communion." That was surely why she always wanted to have a priest nearby and why she bestowed such special care on priests.

For the same reason, she required three guarantees in writing from any bishop who invited her Sisters into his diocese: the right to keep the Most Blessed Sacrament in their chapel and to expose It for Adoration; a priest to be appointed to celebrate Holy Mass every day; and permission to beg for alms in the bishop's diocese.

❧

Mother Teresa was a missionary through and through who saw God's omnipotence and the love of Jesus at work in everything and everyone. At the same time, however, she was also a seeker who marveled, wide-eyed, at the reality and glory of God. I recall a flight that we made together. We were traveling to Prague in a large helicopter. The weather was splendid. The pilot had been asked to fly as low as possible on account of the heart problems that increasingly troubled Mother Teresa. To my great delight he did fly very low; we were able to observe the landscape beneath us in great detail. Mother Teresa sat by the window and looked out, visibly absorbed in God and in marveling at the beautiful landscape. We could see each field, each fence, each street, and each tree quite clearly.

Suddenly she turned to me and said, "Look, Father!" And after a pause: "It's easy to understand God's beauty. Just look down there! It is also easy to understand His omnipotence. He made all this. But it is difficult to understand God's humility." I murmured my agreement but, try as I might, I could not make much sense out of "God's humility."

Years have passed since then. That expression "God's humility" has never left me. Yes, seeing the world from the perspective of God's humility was something entirely new. He is almighty, but He does not impose His omnipotence on us, but rather limits Himself for the sake of our freedom; because of His love for us, God refrains from using His omnipotence. More than that, He becomes helpless, as the Child in the crib and as the Suffering Servant—helpless, even to an ignominious death on the Cross. God does not obtain what is good by force; He takes our wickedness upon Himself as suffering, because without our freedom there cannot be any genuine love. Only when we are free to the point where we can set ourselves against God, does willingness to serve Him have any value. God's humility provides the space for us to be free.

After they have received Holy Communion and the Mass is over, the Sisters in all the houses always say a series of prayers that Mother Teresa not only selected, but also usually led, reciting them in a loud, clear voice.

One of these prayers is by Blessed Cardinal Newman:

> Dear Jesus,
> help us to spread Your fragrance everywhere we go.
> Flood our souls with Your Spirit and life.
> Penetrate and possess our whole being,
> so utterly that our lives may only be a radiance of Yours.
> Shine through us, and be so in us
> that every soul we come in contact with
> may feel Your presence in our soul.
> Let them look up and see no longer us
> but only Jesus!
> Stay with us, and then we shall begin to shine
> as you shine;
> so to shine as to be a light to others;
> the light, O Jesus, will be all from You,
> none of it will be ours;
> it will be You, shining on others through us.
> Let us thus praise You in the way You love best
> by shining on those around us.
> Let us proclaim You without preaching,
> not by words but by our example,
> by the catching force,
> the sympathetic influence of what we do,
> the evident fullness of the love
> our hearts bear to You. Amen.

This idea was central for Mother Teresa: that Jesus radiates from us, shines forth through us, without words.

❧

Especially when children were present, Mother Teresa used to take the opportunity to explain the essence of the Gospel, using the five fingers of one hand: Jesus' identification of Himself with our brothers and sisters, the poorest of the poor. Speaking about the Last Judgment, Jesus Himself says, "As you did it to one of the least of these my brethren, you did it to me" (Mt 25:40). While saying this, Mother Teresa would hold up a child's hand and waggle each of its fingers in turn: "You-did-it-to-me."

Then she had the children repeat: "You did it to me." This one-handed piece of education even had a two-handed continuation: "I will and I want with God's help be holy." This could be counted out on the fingers of both hands.

Every volunteer or coworker who came to Calcutta soon heard the story about the minister from the Indian government who once said to Mother Teresa, "You and I, we both do social work, but there is a big difference between you and us. We do it for some*thing*, and you do it for some*one*."

Mother Teresa used to comment, "I am sure he knew who that 'someone' is."

Once, when Mother Teresa was asked in public whether she was married, she replied, "Yes, I am married to Jesus, but often I find that it is not easy to smile at Him. He can be very demanding." Nevertheless, Mother Teresa did always smile at Him. Perhaps she thought of the rule that she gave her Sisters, who often had no reason to smile: "If you don't smile, *make* a smile!"

For Mother Teresa, belonging to Jesus meant being specifically and unreservedly at God's disposal for His work in the world and allowing oneself to be used by Him for His plans. She used to say that, whatever our abilities, we should make ourselves available for God's work. If we trust completely in Him and in His guidance, then we can succeed in something—even if it is only "not spoiling His work."

She once said this to me quite directly. When I was in Vienna in 1986, the program director of the Austrian Television Network ORF came up with the idea that I should do a televised interview with Mother Teresa. As an amateur I was naturally very nervous, because I had never been in a television studio before. Mother Teresa sensed it: "Father, why are you nervous? Doesn't our life belong entirely to God?"

"Yes, of course," I replied, somewhat ashamed.

"Well, then, we just have to let Him work." After a short pause she added, "The only thing that we have to do is pray that we don't spoil His work! It's His work."

8

Do Little Things with Great Love

I n Mother Teresa's presence, many people realized for the first time how few things in our lives are really necessary, and that a simple lifestyle enables one to manage with very little. It started with clothes; Mother Teresa's sari was patched and darned and had been mended again and again where it had become torn and frayed. The Sisters, however, secretly put her old saris, and sometimes those that were not quite worn out, into a trunk. Although she was general superior, no one told her that her old saris were being collected—the Sisters prudently assumed that these would supply material for the relics that would surely be needed later on.

Eventually, Mother Teresa discovered the trunk and wanted to know what the saris were for. The far-sighted Sisters' clever plan was revealed—and on Mother Teresa's instructions her saris were released again for further use.

Mother Teresa handed on every gift that she received as quickly as possible. Everything always belonged to the poor, the needy, or simply to people who in her view needed a little sign of love at that moment. People who presented her with valuable heirlooms, with the aim of "parking" them near a saint, had miscalculated and were often disappointed. She was an expert at re-gifting. Moreover, she recognized that the complete lack of possessions is also a piece of freedom, and that anything that she could not use immediately was simply a burden.

Once, a well-to-do American heard Mother Teresa speak at a pro-life rally and, impressed by her witness, spontaneously offered her a large house. Mother Teresa asked about the location of the house and whether there were any of the poorest of the poor in that neighborhood. When it turned out that the house was in a fashionable area and was very large, she said that she had no use for it and, with thanks, declined the offer. The generous businessman could not be dissuaded so easily and said that Mother Teresa should accept the house anyway and use it later. She reflected for a moment and then said, "What I cannot use now only burdens me." And after a short pause she said, "If I need something later on, God will help me then."

"It doesn't matter how much we give. It matters how much love we put in the giving." I had been familiar with this saying of Mother Teresa for a long time, and I always found it very beautiful and true. Whenever possible Mother Teresa immediately gave away everything she had.

I have a veritable host of "presents" from her, for example, holy pictures depicting saints I know nothing at all about, a beautiful woolen shawl that she once wrapped around me in the mountains of Central India while she herself froze, holy water fonts, and hand-sized glow-in-the-dark statues of the Blessed Virgin Mary, which she would pull out of her bag in great numbers. With the help of some glue that she also pulled out of her bag, she once glued one of these statues to the windshield of my car, where it accompanied me for many years. If I had not turned away just in time now and then, I would today be the owner of a Czech tea set, crocheted sleeve protectors, a wheelbarrow, and many other useful items.

Last, but not least, there were the Miraculous Medals—by her own admission Mother Teresa gave out at least forty thousand. These medals originated with the appearance of the Mother of God to the saintly nun Catherine Labouré in 1830, when Mary promised great blessings to everyone who wears this medal with faith.

When I think of how gladly and ceaselessly Mother Teresa always tried to give something to everyone she met, a central phrase from the wedding liturgy occurs to me: "Take this ring as a sign of my love and fidelity, in the Name of the Father and of the Son and of the Holy Spirit."

It must have been like that with her. Every present, however small, was a sign of her love for the person who received it. With these little presents, she succeeded in making tiny cracks in our armor of isolation and egoism. And indeed she did "crack open" many people's hearts! She always briefly and firmly clasped the hands of the person to whom she was giving a medal, and the warmth of her hands was a clear expression of her love.

℗

I witnessed a rather scary "armor-cracking" incident with Mother Teresa in Nicaragua, which at that time was ruled by a Marxist-inspired authoritarian regime under the Sandinista leader Daniel Ortega. Mother Teresa requested an opportunity to meet the dictator, so as to obtain permission from him to open a new house for her Sisters. The meeting took place. We were led into a windowless room with a platform at one end. On the platform was a long desk, and behind the desk sat four masked men with big machine guns.

In the middle, between the masked men, sat Daniel Ortega. He gave his three visitors—Mother Teresa, a Sister and me—a fiery, thirty-minute speech about the legitimacy of his guerilla war and the demonic character of his opponents. When he finally ended, trembling with rage, there was an embarrassed silence. Mother Teresa broke it with a single sentence: "Yes, yes, works of love are works of peace."

The tension mounted; the official translator obviously did not want to translate this sentence, which had been spoken in English, into Spanish for the president. Finally, the Sister took on this manifestly thankless task, though in a trembling voice. Not only was the room stifling, there was also a dangerous tension in the air.

Suddenly, and without waiting for the dictator's reaction to her remark, Mother Teresa stood up, went forward and stepped quite close to the platform. Rummaging in her bag, she asked the dictator, "Do you have children?"

Clearly not understanding the implication of her question, he answered, "Yes."

"How many?"

"Seven."

Mother Teresa now brought seven Miraculous Medals out of her bag, one after the other, kissed each one and held it up as high as she could toward the platform. Ortega took them—one by one—leaning far across the desk each time so as to reach Mother Teresa's hand.

"Do you have a wife?"

"Yes!"

Another medal was found in the bag, which was kissed then held out.

"And here's one for you." With that Mother Teresa handed him the last medal. "You need it! But you must wear it round your neck, like this. . ."

Mother Teresa pointed to a cord around the dictator's neck and explained in sign language where the medal should hang.

With one stroke she had completely changed the mood. Then she offered the dictator another present: five of her Sisters to care for the poorest of the poor in the slums of Managua!

Permission was granted the very next day for the founding of the Sisters' first house.

❧

Mother Teresa's congregation of Sisters learned that giving is a sign of love. Years later, I discovered how well they had followed the example of their foundress when the Sisters working in Vienna gave me a securely tied "important" package to take with me on my trip to New York. On it was written, in ornate script: "To the Sisters in New York—with love from Vienna." When I delivered it in New York, I discovered that this important package contained chocolates.

A few weeks later, on my return trip to Vienna, which took me via Washington, I was handed another important package at the Sisters' house in Washington. This time it read: "To the Sisters in Vienna. . ." When the Sisters in Vienna gratefully opened the package, I could not believe my eyes: It was the same box of chocolates that I had taken from Vienna to New York! In the meantime it must have traveled "with love" to Washington and was now traveling back "with love from Washington" across the ocean to Vienna. Then it became clear to me—the present was not the chocolates; the present was the love.

At the Motherhouse in Calcutta there was only one priest for three hundred Sisters, so Mother Teresa and several of the Sisters had permission to help distribute Holy Communion. Once, after she had performed this service during Mass, she took it as a meditation point for the fifteen-minute meditation she frequently gave for the volunteers after Mass. "Today I helped to distribute the Body of Christ. I held the Host with two fingers and thought: How small Jesus made Himself, in order to show us that He doesn't expect great things of us, but rather little things with great love."

❧

I still have in my possession an oversized slab of chocolate that Mother Teresa sent me in Armenia in 1989 as an Easter gift. On the top is the inscription "God bless you, [from] Mother Teresa." To this day I have not eaten the chocolate. It has probably disintegrated into dust inside the wrapper by now, but the love of an extraordinary human being shines from it nevertheless, and it is a lively reminder that "it doesn't matter how much we give. What matters is how much love we put into the giving."

Mother Teresa's ever-watchful attentiveness to her fellow human beings was a consequence of her motto: "Put your love into a living action." I often had the privilege of being the beneficiary of this attentiveness. For example, on the return trip from a university in Central India where Mother Teresa had received an honorary degree, she wanted to take the opportunity to visit two of her foundations that were not far off the route. The local media had announced her visit. On the eight-hour trip back to Madras (today Chennai) the road was almost continuously lined with people who wanted to see Mother Teresa, if only for a moment as she drove by, and to wave to her. The journey was slow because the convoy kept stopping to give village dignitaries the opportunity to greet Mother Teresa.

The sun blazed down mercilessly. There were long speeches. The people crowded round to touch Mother Teresa. At nearly eleven in the evening, when we reached the house of the Sisters in Madras, I was completely exhausted and dehydrated. As always, the first thing we did upon entering was to go to the chapel to say a short, silent thanksgiving prayer before the Most Blessed Sacrament. Even though I probably looked pious, I could not concentrate on "piety," for sheer thirst. I could only think about getting something to drink quickly. Suddenly I heard soft footsteps behind me. Following a signal from Mother Teresa, a Sister had brought me a tiny saucer with a big glass of water on it. She silently pushed it toward my feet from behind.

Ever since then I think of that experience when I read in Saint Matthew's Gospel, "Whoever gives to one of these little ones even a cup of cold water because he is a disciple, truly, I say to you, he shall not lose his reward" (Mt 10:42). Something else became clear to me that day: I had been thinking only about my own thirst; Mother Teresa, however, thought about ours.

Even after our short prayer she still did not think of her own well-being, but instead brought two mattresses, pillows, a washcloth and a piece of soap into the sacristy, so that we two priests who had traveled with her could go to sleep right away. "Now get a good rest. It was a long day for you."

I remarked, "Mother Teresa, it must have been a much longer day for you," but her only reply was a cheerful, yet serious, "All for Jesus!" At seventy-seven years of age she was almost exactly as old as we two priests combined.

A few years later, when asked about her age, she answered with a mischievous glint in her eye, "Outside I'm eighty-one, inside eighteen."

In all the houses of the Missionaries of Charity it is customary for the priest who celebrates the morning Mass to have breakfast afterward—so, too, in Calcutta. Mother Teresa was anxious that Bishop Hnilica, a Slovak priest, a female journalist (who was also Slovak), and I should all have breakfast immediately after Mass—served on a tiny little table in a very narrow sacristy. In the Sisters' houses the sacristy usually served also as a parlor and a reception room. On account of the distinguished episcopal guest, I concluded, Mother Teresa had ordered that each of us should get a fried egg with our breakfast. Given conditions in Calcutta, that was a magnificent gift.

I noticed, though, that not one of the other three touched his fried egg. Each of them had some dietary or other reason for this. So as not to be impolite to the Sisters, and because I really like fried eggs, I "made a sacrifice" and ate all four. The next morning I was the only celebrant at the Mass and afterward had breakfast in the sacristy again. The Bishop and his entourage had other obligations. I was quite astounded when, at breakfast, I lifted the cover from the plate: four fried eggs! Apparently my partiality to fried eggs had not escaped the Sister sacristan. From then on, during my entire stay in Calcutta, every time I celebrated Mass in the morning at the Motherhouse, I got four fried eggs.

Some fifteen years later I gave a retreat in a house of the Sisters near Warsaw. After the morning Mass, breakfast was served in the sacristy; this was the custom there too. To my great surprise, there were four fried eggs. A thought struck me, and my suspicion was quickly confirmed: The Sister who had served me back then in Calcutta had meanwhile become the superior of this house in Poland. She had remembered my predilection for fried eggs. Since then, in many, many parts of the world, I have received four fried eggs. These little acts of thoughtfulness struck me as signs of great love.

And I also realize that the Sisters pass on to one another, from one continent to the next, not only their love but also their little secrets and their knowledge about priests!

Once, Mother Teresa was invited by the mayor of Bonn to receive an award and give a speech. She and her whole entourage were invited to a luncheon that had been prepared in the Rittersaal, a grand and stately hall. Out of consideration for the poorest people in India who, in their generous hospitality, used to offer visitors—including the Sisters when they came to help them—their last piece of bread or handful of rice, Mother Teresa had made it a rule that the Sisters, as a matter of principle, could not eat outside their house, although when traveling they could bring food along and have a picnic. On this occasion, too, Mother Teresa did not allow any exemption from the rule but solved the dilemma in a different way: "Sisters, unpack the food you have brought along. We'll have a picnic here!"

Thereupon, in the venerable Rittersaal, the Sisters distributed their sandwiches to the guests. The mayor and all the other guests at the banquet got the sandwiches that the Sisters had brought with them. Thus the luncheon became a picnic, and the Sisters did not have to break their rule.

In the helicopter on the flight back from Bonn to Prague in a Czech helicopter, Mother Teresa brought all the goodies that she had, as usual, gathered at the reception out of her bag and distributed them to her fellow passengers. Then she brought out a slab of chocolate. You should know that she liked chocolate very much. But before she gave us any, she stood up and went forward to the pilots. After a while she came back again and distributed the rest of the chocolate.

When we had landed, the two Czech pilots disembarked first and stationed themselves to the right and left at the foot of the stairs. Mother Teresa went down the stairs, followed by the other passengers. When I reached the pilots, I saw that one of them had tears in his eyes. I asked him what was the matter. He said, "You know, I've been flying this helicopter for twenty-five years, with many great and famous people as passengers, but I have never received anything from anyone. Today was the first time: Mother Teresa gave me chocolate and a Miraculous Medal."

ℰℭ

In her speech at the United Nations in New York, Mother Teresa told simple little stories, just as she did in all her catechism lessons, in her heavily Indian English, as in the following:

> I never forget, some time ago, two young people came to our house and gave me lots of money. And I asked them, "Where did you get so much money?" And they said, "Two days ago we got married. Before marriage, we decided we will not buy wedding clothes. We will not have [a] wedding feast. We will give you that money." And I know in our country, in a Hindu family, what that means, not to have wedding clothes, not to have a wedding feast. So again I asked, "But why? Why did you do like that?" And they said, "We loved each other so much that we wanted to share the joy of loving with the

people you serve." How do we experience the joy of loving? How do we experience that? By giving until it hurts.

When I was going to Ethiopia, little children [in Calcutta] came to me. They heard I was going there. And they came. They had come to know from the Sisters how much the children are suffering in Ethiopia. And they came and each one gave something, very, very small money. And some, whatever they had, they gave. And a little boy came to me and said, "I have nothing, I have no money, I have nothing. But I have this piece of chocolate. And you give that, take that with you and you give it to the children in Ethiopia." That little child loved with great love, because I think that was the first time that he had a piece of chocolate in his hand. And he gave it. He gave it with joy to be able to share, to remove a little [of] the suffering of someone in far Ethiopia. This is the joy of loving: to give until it hurts. It hurt Jesus to love us, for He died on the cross, to teach us how to love. And this is the way we too must love: until it hurts.[1]

---

[1] Mother Teresa, "One Strong Resolution: I Will Love" (Address to the United Nations on the occasion of its 40th Anniversary, October 26, 1985), http://www.piercedhearts.org/purity_heart_morality/mother_teresa_address_united_nations.htm.

9

With the Poorest of the Poor

MOTHER TERESA, whose given name was Agnes Gonxha Bojaxhiu, was born into a Catholic family of Albanian extraction. Her father, Nikola (Kole) Bojaxhiu, was originally from Prizren. After 1900 he lived in Skopje (then called Üsküp), which today is the capital of Macedonia. He worked there as a pharmacist and then as an architect, until he joined a friend's construction company. Her mother, Drana, was just sixteen years old and eighteen years younger than her husband at the time of their marriage. In 1905 their first child was born, their daughter Aga, and three years later their first son, Lazar. Two years after that, on August 26, 1910, their daughter Agnes came into the world.

In 1910 Skopje was predominantly Muslim with a population of around forty-seven thousand. It had a large Orthodox congregation and a small but self-confident Catholic minority. Skopje had belonged to the Ottoman Empire until the First Balkan War, which began in 1912, and had then become part of Serbia.

Mother Teresa was hardly ever seen without a rosary in her hands. The roots of her devotion can be found in her childhood: Her mother, Drana, took her children with her to Mass in the mornings and prayed the Rosary with them in the evenings. It was here too that little Agnes learned about the social dimension of her Faith; her mother used to visit the sick and the poor. Agnes' family was quite prosperous until her father died at the age of forty-six. Kole Bojaxhiu was interested in political issues, stood up for the rights of Albanians, and became a member of the city council. In 1919 he returned from a meeting in the Serbian capital, Belgrade, with severe pains, was brought to a hospital in Skopje, and died a few hours later. His son Lazar was always convinced that his father had been poisoned for political reasons.

After her father's death, Mother Teresa and her family fell on very tough times. Her mother worked hard as a seamstress to keep the family afloat. With her mother's approval, Agnes left the family at the age of eighteen to join the Loreto Sisters in Ireland and to dedicate her life to the missions as Sister Teresa. In 1934 her mother and sister moved from Skopje to the Albanian capital, Tirana; she never saw them again. Despite repeated interventions, sometimes by high-ranking politicians, Communist Albania would not allow Mother Teresa to enter the country until its political collapse.

Skopje is not only Mother Teresa's physical birthplace, but also the cradle of her spiritual vocation. In 1922, at the age of twelve, Agnes heard Croatian Jesuits who worked in India preach for the first time. From that time on she felt an increasing desire to go to India as a missionary. Agnes and her sister Aga belonged to a parish group of the Children of Mary organization in the Jesuit-run parish of the Sacred Heart. This certainly left an impression, for throughout her life her spirituality was Marian, Jesuit-influenced and focused on the Heart of Jesus.

The Loreto Sisters in Dublin were also strongly influenced by the Jesuits, and she turned to them with the express aim of going to India as a missionary. The Irish branch of the Loreto Sisters had been founded in 1822 as the Mary Ward Sisters by Teresa Ball (1794–1861) in Rathfarn-ham near Dublin.

In late 1928, Agnes finally arrived in India as a novice with the Loreto Sisters and immersed herself completely and utterly in the country, learning Bengali and some Hindi. An Indian journalist once said to her, "Mother Teresa, you are not a native Indian at all, but you are a nationalized Indian." She replied: "I'm more Indian than you. I decided to be an Indian. You had no choice at all."

☙

After an arduous flight from Europe, usually with a stopover in Delhi or Bombay, you finally arrive in Calcutta. Once your passport has been checked and you have been through the customs formalities, you are hit by the hot, humid wave of air from the entrance to the airport. But what strikes you even more than the heat is a sound that you soon recognize as the screaming and yelling of hundreds of children waiting at the entrances, hoping for a tip or a gift of some kind. If, in that sweltering air and noise, you manage to fight your way through the confusion to a taxi, and to climb into one of the antiquated yellow-and-black cars, you have successfully completed the first stage.

Sometimes it is not so easy to get the taxi driver to understand where you really want to go. Of course, before you get in, the driver always insists that he is well acquainted with the destination that you give. But as soon as you are sitting in the taxi, things look quite different. Often this is the beginning of a random drive lasting for hours, unless you yourself happen to know the way.

Mother Teresa had graciously made arrangements for Bishop Hnilica and me to stay with the Jesuits on Park Street. My room was an extension built onto the roof terrace, and it was so hot that the windows had to be kept open all the time. As a result the room was covered, completely covered, in Calcutta's dust, and the air was polluted with car and factory emissions. Even though I was well equipped with a variety of cleaning products that I had brought with me from Europe, and was also quite prepared to scrub and clean, I must confess that I did not even begin in that room. The hopelessness of the undertaking was clear. Instead of applying detergents, I limited myself to handling as little as possible. I turned the water faucet on and off again carefully with two fingers.

Every morning I got up at 4:15 at the call of the muezzin and walked for twenty minutes through the streets to the Motherhouse. The people who slept on the pavements were also getting up, to begin their morning ablutions. For many of them this consisted of washing out their loincloth in the foam-covered rivulet that crept slowly through the gutter, and beating it dry on the pavement until they could put it on again. They pushed aside the poisonous white foam with their index fingers, wet the fingers, and ritually cleaned all their teeth three times. Now I understood why many people, especially the elderly and the sick, could not get up at all in the mornings and thus became patients in Mother Teresa's houses, especially in the House for the Dying. They were brought there either to get well, or else to die as human beings where they would be loved and cared for.

In 1984, the first time I came to Calcutta, together with Bishop Hnilica and a Slovak journalist, Mother Teresa immediately had the Bishop and me measured for new white cassocks. These were ready early the next morning. They were ideal in that heat since they were lightweight and easy to wash. The thin fabric of the cassock dried overnight because the climate in Calcutta is mainly dry and hot. Yet Mother Teresa did this less out of concern for our health or our laundry, than to make sure that people would immediately recognize us as priests.

I was privileged to experience this again and again. For Mother Teresa, the essential thing about me was not some quality or skill of mine, nor a character trait or a connection, but the fact that I was a priest. And at the same time she wanted to shape me as a priest. That is why she allowed me to be close to her and around the Sisters. To use a priest for his specific ministry and at the same time to shape him—these were two sides of the same coin. For example, when people would crowd around her and ask her for a blessing—"Mother, your blessing!"—she always sent them on to the priest as well, if there happened to be one within reach: "Let Father bless you, too!"

℘

Mother Teresa usually had me lodge with the Jesuits in Calcutta. Sometimes, when no other room was free, I was put in the extension on the roof terrace. As might be expected, it was hot there, both day and night. There was a ceiling fan, and the bed had netting; every evening I had to lie down very carefully in the bed and tuck the netting all around under the mattress, so as not to become a pincushion for the ever-present mosquitoes. But, despite all my precautionary measures, I awoke the first morning with an arm full of bug bites. I was annoyed and resolved to check the netting very carefully that night. And I did, but the following morning my forearms were again covered with bites. On the fourth day they were already inflamed.

When I arrived at the Motherhouse at 5:30 that morning, together with a stream of volunteers, Mother Teresa immediately picked me out of the crowd. "Father, what do you have there?"

"Probably mosquito bites."

She looked more closely: "A gift of God! Father, go to the doctor now—and I will pray."

Later I understood that for her any adversity, pain or suffering could be a "gift of God." Anything, in fact, that through a little act of the will, could be transformed into a "gift to God." What struck me ever after that morning was this particular attentiveness that she always had to her surroundings—even to the smallest detail. She sensed it when someone who came in was sad or in pain; she tried to help in any way that she could: through deeds, through words, or—if nothing else was possible—through prayer.

The Sister who treated the inflammation gave me a tip: when I woke up I should look under the cushions. The next morning I snatched the cushions away and saw eight fat bedbugs! I squashed each one through the bed sheet. (Animal rights activists will surely make allowances.) Eight big spots of blood! The bedbugs had been living in the mattress and feeding on my blood.

At that time, some three hundred Sisters were living in the Motherhouse in Calcutta. There was only one source of water, located on the first floor. If you stood at the entrance to the chapel, several stories up, and looked down over the railing, you saw an "anthill"—three hundred Sisters swarming around every day, pumping water and washing their saris, either in complete silence or accompanied by hymns.

Always, though, you could feel great happiness. I often stood by the railing for a long time and looked down to take in the atmosphere of poverty in which the Sisters lived. Mother Teresa always used to say: "In order to understand the poor, we ourselves must live the life of the poor." There, looking down over the railing, you could at least begin to understand. The Sisters had no radio, no television, no air conditioner. The only fans they had were for their patients and their visitors—not for themselves. They lived the life of the poor, with one difference: they had chosen it freely and for Jesus' sake.

10

Contemplatives in the World

MOTHER TERESA has become a symbol of Christian charity and compassion for the whole world. Her name is almost synonymous with tender loving care for the poorest among us. Many people have asked what the essential core of Mother Teresa's secret was. Everyone who knew her really well agrees that the Eucharist—both at Mass and at daily Adoration—played a very special role for her.

Regarding her secret, she answered a question clearly once on a journey in Italy. A young priest had just prayed the Liturgy of the Hours and the Rosary with Mother Teresa and her traveling companions. They had scarcely finished when he spontaneously asked, "Mother Teresa, what is your secret?" She looked at him with a quizzical twinkle in her eye and replied, "That's very simple: I pray."

After my ordination to the priesthood and my first encounters with Mother Teresa, I was very interested in her spirituality. I made a thirty-day silent retreat in the house of the Missionaries of Charity Fathers (a branch of the Missionaries of Charity Family) in New York to discern whether I should join them. At that time Mother Teresa was often at the Fathers' new house in New York, since they were discussing the statutes.

After my retreat, I told Mother Teresa that a Capuchin Father had warned me, right at the beginning of my priestly vocation: "Don't think that you can be a priest without praying at least an hour and a half each day!" I had been very impressed at the time, but I had not really understood the significance of lengthy prayer. Now I wanted to understand what prayer meant to Mother Teresa. Her answer was simple and clear: "Father, without God we are too poor to help the poor, but when we pray, God places His love in us. Look, the Sisters are poor, but they pray. The fruit of prayer is love. The fruit of love is service. Only when you pray can you really serve the poor."

I remember once at a gas station, during a trip we were making together, she looked for a long time at the nozzle through which the gas was flowing into the tank and then said, "Look, Father, that's like blood in the body: Without blood there is no life in the body. Without gas in the car—no driving. But also, without prayer the soul is dead."

One of Mother Teresa's standard sayings was that "prayer gives us a pure heart. It purifies our heart. And a pure heart can see God." I did not understand right away what it meant to see God. But for her, "seeing God" was the ability to recognize God's presence and His workings in our own life, to perceive His hand in everything, and to respond to these divine workings with our love. She once said, "If you have a pure heart, you can see God in every thing and in every person."

From that she then deduced: "If we see God, we will love one another as God loves us." That is why the motto of her life was "Love in action."

ဢ

When I saw Mother Teresa pray, often pressing her hands right into her face, pressing her nose upward in her profound absorption, it reminded me of the words of Jesus' disciples who saw the Lord praying and asked Him, "Lord, teach us also to pray." And then Jesus taught them the Our Father.

When asked what prayer was for her, Mother Teresa answered: "God speaks to me—and I speak to Him. It's that simple. That is prayer." Prayer is heart-to-heart contact. "If I pray to Jesus, then it's from my heart to Jesus' Heart. When I pray to the Mother of God, then it's from my heart to Mary's heart. When I pray to my guardian angel, then it's also heart to heart." Mother Teresa's central principle with regard to prayer was this: "God speaks in the silence of our heart, and we listen. Then, out of the fullness of our heart, we speak and He listens. And that is prayer."

"Prayer doesn't happen by itself," Mother Teresa once said. "We have to make the effort to pray." She did not teach complicated prayer techniques, but always reminded people that we must be conscious of what we are doing when we pray, and that we must pay attention. Then prayer happens, deep in the heart.

For Mother Teresa, prayer was childlike contact, like the contact of a child with his father—never superficial, just "heart to heart."

In Mother Teresa's spirituality, prayer is the human response to God's yearning as expressed in Jesus' cry on the Cross, "I thirst!" And when she spoke about her houses, she said simply, "We gave Jesus a new tabernacle," for although she selected and set up her houses very pragmatically, a new house without the Blessed Sacrament was inconceivable to her. One felt that, in her opinion, there should be at least one tabernacle in every part of the world. She decided exactly where the tabernacle would be in her houses, she hammered the nail for the crucifix into the wall herself, and she cut out the letters that made up "I THIRST" in black paper. She was convinced that a person can satisfy his longing for the Son of God by being with Him, in His presence, in silence.

For Mother Teresa, prayer did not just consist of praying at set times. Like Paul, she taught that we must "pray at all times" (Eph 6:18). In her case this "pray[ing] at all times" took the form of the rosary that she held constantly in her hand and also constantly "used." I often observed how she would let the beads of the rosary slip quickly through her fingers.

I remember, for instance, a trip that we made together to the mountains of Central India where a university was being inaugurated. I was sitting on a step right beneath her, and my eyes were at the level of her hands with the rosary. For hours I was able to watch how she continuously drew the beads through her fingers, but at a speed that was obviously too fast to recite a Hail Mary for each bead. I decided to ask her what prayers she said at that speed. But sadly I still don't know; I never plucked up the courage to ask her. Something held me back, and I can only speculate on the contents of that high-speed prayer. I suspect that she said an aspiration on each rosary bead, a short prayer such as "My Jesus, mercy" or "Jesus, Son of God, have mercy on me."

I was already a priest, but still studying missiology in Rome, when I once asked her, "Mother Teresa, your speech in Oslo when you were awarded the Nobel Prize impressed many people. Dissertations are now being written about it at universities. How did you prepare it? What kind of resources did you use? Did anyone help you write it?"

Mother Teresa said nothing, unfastened her rosary from her belt, held it high like a flag and waved it back and forth in front of my eyes with an incredibly impish gleam in her eyes.

Prayer, and indeed Mother Teresa's whole spiritual life, especially the sacraments, were the foundation of her worldwide apostolate. I am sure that I know the main reason why I often had the privilege of accompanying her: She needed a priest who would celebrate Mass every day for her and her Sisters and hear their confessions.

The Sisters spend at least an hour each day in Adoration before the Blessed Sacrament exposed in the chapel. In 1972 when a catastrophic flood struck Bangladesh, Mother Teresa immediately sent her Sisters there to help out. The needs were enormous, and the work demanded superhuman efforts on the part of the Sisters. So they were asked if they would make an exception and not interrupt their work for their prayer sessions.

Mother Teresa decided against it: "No, the Sisters will come home for Adoration and Holy Mass." Many of the relief workers who had responded to the catastrophic flood did not understand, but for Mother Teresa it was clear that the Sisters' strength dries up if they are not nourished daily by Mass and their Adoration of the Holy Eucharist.

Her constant witness was the result of her constant prayer. It struck me on many journeys and drives with Mother Teresa that there was never a time when she was not a consecrated religious and, most importantly, a herald of Jesus' love. When I accompanied her, wearing my priest's collar and in my official capacity, I would always withdraw at some point. As soon as I was home, or could lie down in one of the Sisters' guest rooms, I was unavailable to anyone for a while. Of course I did not stop being a priest, but I let my active witness take a back seat to my own weariness or my own need for rest and relaxation. With Mother Teresa, whether she was sick or sitting in a wheelchair, whether she was at an airport or staying with her Sisters, there seemed to be no such withdrawal. She was so thoroughly imbued with the experience of God's yearning for our love that she could never place her own needs first.

I would even venture to say that she could not handle bread without thinking of the Eucharist. In her view, physical hunger and other sorts of neediness were always the expression of our hunger for Christ. She showed in her daily life that our life here on earth is embedded in eternal life.

෴

Mother Teresa quoted the saying, "The family that prays together, stays together" countless times. This saying, with which she has become identified, did not originate with her but with Father Patrick Payton, an American Holy Cross Father and a renowned apostle of family prayer. Mother Teresa made this saying her own, for prayer and loving unity in the family were very dear to her heart. Again and again she asked people, "Where does love begin?" and then gave the answer herself: "Love begins at home, in the family."

Father Brian Kolodiejchuk has quoted Mother Teresa as follows:

> The family is a special instrument in God's hands, for it is chiefly through the family that God wants to tell us that we are created for greater things: to love and to be loved. As our families are, so will our relations with our neighbors be, and

so will our towns, cities and our whole country appear. If the family becomes a place of love and peace and holiness, then our nations and our world too will live in love, in peace and in unity with God and with each other.[1]

In many cities throughout the world, the Sisters look after people who are elderly and helpless. The houses are always very simply furnished but completely clean, and the elderly people are remarkably cheerful with each other and with the Sisters. I mentioned this once to Mother Teresa and she said, "Father, why do you think that in so many retirement homes all the people sit by the entrance and look at the door?"

Since I had no answer, Mother Teresa explained: "Perhaps because their sons and daughters put them in that home, where they have all the material things that they need. But in reality they have been forgotten there by their children. Do you see elderly people smiling in those homes? Often they are the poorest of the poor, because they have a great hunger, a hunger for love. We must always ask ourselves: Don't we have some of the poorest of the poor in our own family? And we must remember that charity begins at home."

Yes, in the family we experience what it means when Jesus says about Himself that He is the Way, the Truth and the Life. In Mother Teresa's words: "What is true for each individual is also true for the family: When the family listens to Jesus' word, it hears the Truth. When we obey His commandments, we follow Jesus, Who is the Way. When we receive His sacraments, we live Jesus, Who is the Life."

---

[1] Personal communication, 2002.

11

Disarmingly Charming

B ECAUSE OF MOTHER TERESA'S OWN KINDNESS and self-discipline, the people around her became self-disciplined and never superficial. Through the way in which she greeted people and paid attention to them, she changed the atmosphere in every room she entered. I will never forget how she herself would always fetch extra chairs to make sure that everyone had somewhere to sit. And when you visited her, you always had the impression that she had been waiting for no one else.

During my first encounters with her, I attributed this to the fact that I was in the entourage of a bishop. But in fact, she always greeted everybody with a beaming smile, regardless of rank or social status. She radiated an inner joy toward everyone that usually toppled any prejudices or resentments that may have been present. I experienced this later with several people whom I took along to see Mother Teresa, whether for morning Mass or for a short conversation. Some of these people even wanted absolutely nothing to do with the Church. Nevertheless, they were enfolded and warmed by their first encounter, so that everything that was cold in them melted and they emerged from the conversation, sometimes after only ten minutes, completely changed.

Yes, Mother Teresa had a naturally very winning personality, but at least as strong, if not stronger, was her influence at a spiritual level, and the two were completely intertwined. Many people were convinced that she had the gift of "reading hearts," in other words, she could look into a person's heart and spontaneously tell them things that she absolutely could not have known by any natural means.

❧

Once, Mother Teresa went to Spain, where she was driven around by a young man named Pascual, who at that time managed a travel agency but later became a priest. She was looking for a house for her Spanish AIDS orphans, which she eventually got in record time through a series of "coincidences." Mother Teresa's Sisters still care for AIDS orphans in that house.

Pascual was a lively travel agent who traveled all over the world. After taking Mother Teresa to the airport in Madrid, he asked her to autograph a book for him as they said goodbye to each other. In the confusion of the departure he had no opportunity to look and see what she had written for him. Only later, when he was back at his apartment, did he open the book. Her dedication began with the words "Dear Father Pascual." He was alarmed. Apparently, she had mistaken him the whole time for a priest!

Pascual hid the book on the shelf behind other books. He wanted to spare himself the ridicule that he was sure the dedication would elicit from his friends.

Thus hidden, the book was forgotten—until ten years later he sorted through his books, found the volume from Mother Teresa, opened it up and read her dedication. Meanwhile, something that he would have considered unthinkable a decade earlier had happened: He had become a priest.

Mother Teresa was always well aware of authority and its importance—priestly, episcopal and papal authority, but also her own authority as general superior. In cases where she herself had to decide something, she made a clear distinction between "decision making" and "decision taking," in other words, between the gathering of the different aspects and the final taking of the decision. On her way to a decision she consulted many people, asked their advice and studied the issues with great attention and concentration. But as soon as she felt that she had all the elements assembled, the only thing left was prayer—and then she decided. Her decision then stood firm as a rock. It was then that she was "the benevolent dictator," as many people called her.

When it was a question of the ecclesiastical authorities, she knew precisely what to ask the Pope about and what she should refer to the local bishop. She also took the advice of every single priest very seriously. I remember that one priest said to me, "We have to be careful what we advise her to do. She actually does it!" Indeed, she gave due weight to good quality information, especially when it came from clergymen and consecrated religious. For her, a priest was someone who has a special relationship with Christ, not because of his individual gifts or talents, but by virtue of his ordination. Whether or not he himself was always conscious of this was quite irrelevant. Even if he did not take the dignity of his priesthood seriously, Mother Teresa took his answers seriously, because she attributed a special role to priests in discerning God's will.

❧

When Mother Teresa returned from a trip, we always wanted to know, not only everything that she had done and accomplished, but also, naturally, what difficulties she had run into and any mean things or nasty tricks that the high-ranking politicians or officials she had met had done. In short, we wanted to hear the spicy stories, too.

But Mother Teresa, as a matter of principle, never said a negative word about anyone. In response to our eager questions about whether she had been betrayed here or there, whether they had hoodwinked, manipulated or mistreated her, she usually replied, "They were so good to us!" Instead of the hoped-for spicy stories, she told us how her hosts, or the governments in the countries where she had been traveling, had helped with this and that, the efforts that they had made and the successes that had resulted.

Never was there a negative word, so that once someone said, "But, Mother Teresa, surely not everything went well."

Her answer came without hesitation: "You know, Father: rather excuse than accuse." I remember hearing her say this several times. On another occasion—in Moscow, after experiences with the Soviet authorities that were certainly not always pleasant—we pressed her again, but even then we got no derogatory remarks, only a lesson: "If you judge someone, then you have no time to love him."

An Indian family who had helped her a lot at the beginning of her work in the slums of Calcutta had a very special place in their hearts for Mother Teresa, so she used to go back regularly to visit that family. It is reported that on one of those visits the daughter, now an adult, was also present and she suddenly began to complain to Mother Teresa about the corruption in the Calcutta administration. You needed a bribe for everything; you couldn't get anything done without greasing palms. She wanted Mother Teresa, who had a very good reputation with the Calcutta administration, to put in a good word for a friend of hers. The young woman said, "Mother Teresa, can't you help us? Calcutta is so corrupt. You get nothing unless you bribe people."

Mother Teresa reacted as she usually did when people "were speaking darkness," as she put it, or when someone "was spreading darkness": "Yes, they're wonderful people. They have given us so much support for our children."

The young woman would not be content with that and retorted, "Mother Teresa, the great majority of people in Calcutta are just running after money."

For the second time, Mother Teresa tried to introduce a hopeful note, and she spoke about the Hindu custom of always putting a handful of rice at the door for the poor.

The young woman was exasperated: "Mother Teresa, when will you wake up? Calcutta is a hell of corruption."

There were a few seconds of painful silence. Mother Teresa remained quite calm, looked the young woman right in the eyes and said, "I know very well that there is corruption in Calcutta, but I also know that there is good, and I have decided to see the good."

Mother Teresa was not so naïve as not to see the evil. Instead it was a deliberate act, a conscious decision to live in love and hope. And it was also a very conscious decision to believe in the good in people.

The Sisters used to joke that Mother Teresa would even make excuses for the devil. Again and again she emphasized that you shouldn't listen to all the negative stories about anyone.

It is much better to pray for them. She once remarked, "One sin that I have never had to confess is that I judged someone."

Clearly she had very thoroughly learned the lesson that her mother had taught her three children in Skopje. At home, whenever the children grumbled about a teacher, the mother would turn the electricity off. As she succinctly explained, "I'm not going to pay for electricity for children who bad-mouth people."

Mother Teresa wanted to help people, not accuse or judge them. So she helped the poor, the drug addicts and the AIDS patients. She helped Hindus and Muslims and also Christians and atheists, when they were dying. Her love knew no boundaries; she made no distinctions as to race or religion, social status or worldview. In that way she showed us what Christian love of our neighbor is supposed to be.

It was a mystery to me how Mother Teresa coped with all the accusations and charges that were leveled at her, especially from England and also by many German authors. She herself once gave us the answer when she spoke about dealing with insults: "If someone accuses you, ask yourself first: Is he right? If he's right, go and apologize to him. If he's not right, then take the insult that you have received in both hands. Don't let it go but seize the opportunity and give it to Jesus as a sacrifice. Be glad that you have something valuable to give Him."

She was conscious at every moment of the fact that God is love, that this love embraces all people, and that she herself and all of us are only fragile instruments in God's hand. That is why she always used to say, "Let us pray that we don't spoil God's work." She was firmly, unshakably convinced that all the good that happens is His work!

As AIDS increasingly became a topic in the media, there were certainly voices claiming that this new plague was a punishment from God for sin, or at least in some sense a consequence of sin. So I listened with great interest when someone asked Mother Teresa, "Mother Teresa, is the AIDS epidemic the result of sin?"

Mother Teresa looked the questioner in the eyes and said, "I, Mother Teresa, am a sinner. We are all sinners. And we all need God's mercy." I recalled Mother Teresa's remark: "One sin that I have never had to confess is that I judged someone."

When we were in Prague, Mother Teresa told me about the founding of the Missionaries of Charity Fathers in New York on October 31, 1984. This, her fifth religious congregation, consisted of priests who would serve as Missionaries of Charity. At first there were only five. They all made a special promise to her never to say a disparaging word about anyone, either within the congregation or outside it. Mother Teresa commented, "As priests you must be there exclusively for Jesus. No one and nothing must come between you and Jesus." Then she gave me another bit of pastoral advice. In order to renew a parish, it is good to have, as Jesus did, "a team of eight, ten or twelve people who really want to bring Christ into the parish."

❧

Often, in order to plan trips or to report on a trip, I had to call Mother Teresa in Calcutta. One thing struck me from the start: She herself almost always picked up the receiver. Sometimes I delayed my calls because I felt that I would just be stealing valuable time from her with my reports or questions. But she always managed to dispel my anxiety with three or four cheerful words.

My younger sister was a volunteer in Calcutta for several months. Every time I called, Mother Teresa told me how kindly my sister behaved toward the poor and how much she loved them: "We will see what God wants for her!" Was that perhaps a little hint or a hope that she would enter the community? At any rate, I remember that I was always very proud when Mother Teresa praised my sister.

I mentioned right at the beginning of this book that Mother Teresa reminded me a lot of my own grandmother, partly because of her many wrinkles but more because of her warmth and the direct way in which she approached people. When she turned to speak to someone, she concentrated on them completely. It was as if she and that person, with their questions and concerns, were the only people there. I noticed something similar in Pope John Paul II.

So she did not regard visitors as a bothersome disturbance. For that moment, whether it lasted seconds or minutes or even hours, that individual was, for Mother Teresa, the most important person in the world. Through this feeling of being accepted by her and, indeed, important to her, and through this intimacy, many people who met her felt that they were her best friend. After her death I discovered that very many people felt this.

In Pondichéry (today, Puducherry), the part of India that was once a French colony and where French missionaries had worked, a woman once told me, "The missionaries brought us a new religion, a third religion besides Buddhism and Hinduism. Mother Teresa brought us the love of Christ."

12

How to Grab a Bull by the Horns

THE COURAGE that I always admired in Mother Teresa seemed to be not only one of her great virtues, but also part of her nature. One example is that when she was still a teacher at the Loreto Sisters' school in Calcutta, she is said to have gone for a walk one day with her pupils through a large meadow. Suddenly, a snorting bull came running toward them. The girls fled screaming and the bull stormed after them. Mother Teresa took a red umbrella, opened it, and went straight up to the bull. Apparently, the animal was so startled that it turned around and trotted off. This may only be a myth but, on the other hand, there would be no myth if the bull had decided on another course of action.

Many years later, in Sandinista-ruled Nicaragua, I myself had the opportunity to marvel at Mother Teresa's courage. She planned to open a house for her Sisters in the capital, Managua. I have already mentioned how she succeeded in bringing her Sisters into Communist Nicaragua by negotiating directly with the Sandinista leader Daniel Ortega. At that time the situation between the Catholic Church and the Sandinista regime, which took Marx, Lenin and especially Fidel Castro as its inspiration, was so tense that no one could guarantee our safety.

It was said that Marian apparitions were taking place a few hours' drive from Managua, in a place called Cuapa. Cardinal Miguel Obando y Bravo, the local bishop, regarded these favorably. A big festival was due to take place in Cuapa. We set out in a convoy of cars, led by the police, and traveled along hazardous roads and paths flooded by streams up into the mountains that surrounded Cuapa. The final kilometers were lined with white stones—the symbol of the political opposition to the government.

The visionary, Bernardo, to whom Mary was said to appear, greeted us and told us all about the apparitions. Then there was a picnic in a big meadow. There were several bishops in our group, including Cardinal Darío Castrillon Hoyos, then president of the Central American Bishops' Conference, and the aforementioned archbishop of Managua (Cardinal Bravo). Suddenly, a hundred heavily armed soldiers emerged from the nearby woods. Even though I did not know who they were or to what unit they belonged, I felt extremely uneasy.

As in the story about the bull, Mother Teresa took the initiative. The soldiers had just taken up a threatening position when she stood up and walked straight toward them. She stopped right in front of their machine guns, which were aimed at us. She rummaged in her bag and gave each soldier a Miraculous Medal, one by one. In order to take the medals, the soldiers had to sling their weapons round their necks. After Mother Teresa had given a medal to each and every soldier—and they had taken them—she invited them all to eat with us. They declined. We were able to proceed more or less calmly to our picnic. A few days later Mother Teresa received permission to bring her Sisters to Managua.

ↀ

Several months later I received a request from Mother Teresa; she asked whether I could also go to Cuba to give a retreat to the Sisters there. She was convinced that as a citizen of neutral Austria I could get a visa relatively easily: "Father, just go to the embassy. They'll give you the visa!" I had my misgivings; normally you had to apply for a visa in your home country or at one of the major consulates. A European could not usually get a visa for a neighboring Communist country at the smaller embassies. So I made my way rather glumly past the high hedges of the Cuban embassy in Managua and past the guards. I presented my request for a visa to Cuba, waited several hours, and was then told that they could not give me a visa and that I should try again the next day. So I went back the next day. Again the answer was no. The following day they told me that, although I could not get a visa there, I would be able to get one in Washington, D.C. or New York. Disheartened, I left the embassy building.

By the hedge stood an elderly woman who tugged at my sleeve and said, "Come, come with me!" She pulled me into a side entrance to the building, gave me a slip of paper on which was written "C-16," and said, "Be at the airport at four this afternoon. You can come on our flight." I thanked her and left, but I did not understand what was going on. Who was that woman? What did she want? Even if she intended to help me, I was convinced that she must have made a mistake. It was Wednesday, and there was no flight to Havana on a Wednesday.

Nevertheless I got to the airport punctually with my small bag—you never know. Standing on the tarmac were two small airplanes and a jet airliner. I went to the check-in and showed my passport and the square slip of paper with the number on it that the woman had given me. When she saw it, the stewardess sent me to another exit where there was another checkpoint. I showed my slip of paper again, and suddenly found myself in a line of elderly women, real Communist babushkas, loaded down with handbags and bulging plastic bags, who were walking through the exit and straight across the airfield to the airliner. Someone signaled that I should join them. I ended up sitting with my bag somewhere among the babushkas—I assume in Row 16, Seat C. As soon as the last person had boarded, the plane took off.

After a short flight we landed in Havana. Again I followed the babushkas, but feeling rather depressed since I still had no Cuban visa. The ladies headed for a side entrance beside the usual airport terminal. There was a policeman standing at a fence. No one checked my passport. And so suddenly, against all expectations and without a visa, I was standing in Fidel Castro's kingdom. There was no one to pick me up since I had not informed the Sisters that I was coming—indeed, I myself had not thought it would happen. Later, the Vatican Nuncio in Cuba explained to me that there are irregular flights that take the wives of Cuban politicians to Nicaragua for shopping sprees.

Mother Teresa had met Fidel Castro some months before and offered him her Sisters for the poorest of the poor and for the dying in his country. Astonishingly, he had accepted. And so the Sisters had come to Cuba to care for the poorest of the poor and especially for the dying. But when I gave the retreat, it turned out that the Sisters were only allowed to work in one hospital, and even there only on one ward—and for just one dying man.

All four Sisters, therefore, were focused on this one man. This absolutely bizarre restriction had been imposed on them, not by Fidel Castro, but by the director of the hospital. As a result the Missionaries of Charity were somewhat despondent. But their superior consoled them: "If Jesus wants to concentrate so much love on one dying man, then he must certainly need it." This thought enabled them to endure the long weeks in which they were only allowed to care for that one man.

Later, the Sisters' permit was extended and they were allowed to buy a building. However, there were long-term residents still living there, and of course the Sisters did not want to throw them out. This led to a difficult situation, because the Sisters had to leave their old house but could not yet move into the new one because of the existing tenants.

Moreover, they could not pursue their normal apostolate of visiting the lonely and the sick outside the hospital, because visits from "foreign" Sisters would have put the families they visited at risk. (The children seemed unaware of this rule and came in droves to the Missionary Sisters.) Every contact with foreigners was a dangerous offense in totalitarian Communist regimes. When I told Mother Teresa about this situation, she simply said, "Then the Sisters should visit as many families as possible; they cannot lock them all up."

13

Souls in Need

THE CONGREGATION that Mother Teresa had founded had grown enormously since its beginnings. In the first few years, the poorest of the poor whom the Missionaries of Charity cared for were mainly people who were materially poor; after independence and the subsequent partition of India in 1947, millions of refugees had transformed Calcutta into a city of human misery.

In that year, approximately ten million Hindus and Sikhs were driven out of the newly established Islamic Republic of Pakistan, and around seven million Muslims out of India. Almost a million people lost their lives fleeing and living as refugees in these tragic expulsions. In that same year, the first Indo-Pakistani War began. India staggered from one famine to the next, and the human misery became immense.

Yet Mother Teresa very soon saw that there was also material need in the wealthy countries of the world and that there was, in addition, a much less visible misery: a poverty that could not be relieved with a bowl of rice. "When someone is lonely or abandoned, when he is without a job or unwanted, rejected and an outcast from society," she often explained, "then this is a form of poverty that is much more difficult to eliminate than hunger. This poverty is found even in the richest countries of the world."

That is why Mother Teresa brought her Sisters into many major cities in the West, for example, Rome, London, New York and Vienna. Nor did it escape her notice that, besides these two forms of poverty, there was a third form, namely, spiritual poverty, which goes much deeper than hunger or loneliness. This spiritual poverty is found in people who are without God, in people who have no faith and who often do not even have the opportunity to hear about faith or to practice it freely.

🙢

In Nirmal Hriday, the House for the Dying in Calcutta, the material poverty was very great. And working there was not easy for the volunteers. In the beginning of their time as volunteers there, many people found it hard to look after the dying, but neither was it particularly pleasant scrubbing floors or cleaning toilets. There was not much competition for those chores! The volunteers' reluctance meant that the Sisters or Mother Teresa herself often cleaned the toilets.

Perhaps for educational reasons—who knows?—a story went round there about something that had happened years earlier, which illuminates the connection between spiritual and material poverty from an unusual perspective. An elegantly dressed man came into the House for the Dying and asked to speak with Mother Teresa. The Sisters informed him that Mother Teresa was at the back of the house cleaning the toilets. So he walked in the direction they had indicated and found Mother Teresa literally scrubbing the toilets. She saw him come in, evidently took him for a volunteer, and immediately explained to him how to hold the toilet brush correctly and how to clean the toilet so as to conserve water. Then she put the brush in his hand and left him standing there.

After fifteen minutes the man came back from the room, went straight up to Mother Teresa and said, "I have finished; may I speak with you now?"

"Yes, certainly," Mother Teresa replied.

He took an envelope out of his pocket and said, "Mother Teresa, I am the director of the airline, and here are your tickets. I just wanted to bring them to you personally."

That airline director later recounted the incident again and again, saying, "Those were the most important twenty minutes of my life—cleaning toilets." He said he had never experienced such joy as on that day.

Four workers whom Mother Teresa "recruited" quite spontaneously also experienced the joy of being able to help. Mother Teresa was setting up a meal at a soup kitchen where she always volunteered, and she needed a few strong arms to move a heavy crate. She opened the door, went out into the street, looked around and asked four men to come in and help her. Once the work was done, it emerged that two of the men were pallbearers and the other two road workers. All four left the place beaming and equipped with Miraculous Medals.

 c/ɔ

The Sisters' first accommodation in Vienna was located in a district where many poor people live. Very soon, it was overflowing with homeless and needy people and the Sisters needed to look for a bigger house. As soon as she arrived in Vienna, Mother Teresa asked for a list of people who could help her look for one. Then she sat down at the telephone and called them one by one. After a short time she found two managers from the world of business who said that they would buy a house for Mother Teresa and let her have it for one dollar per year.

The house was located in a red light district and had been used as a brothel until shortly before it was sold. Mother Teresa wanted to see it right away to decide whether it would be any use to the Sisters. I wondered secretly: Will Mother Teresa refuse to go in? And how will she behave in the house?

To my surprise she entered the house like any other building and looked around. Only I felt rather uneasy because of the pictures on the wall and the smell and I was ashamed, as though I was partly responsible for Mother Teresa having to see it all. She, however, seemed not to notice the furnishings and pictures at all, but went from room to room saying, "So, this will be the chapel, the tabernacle will go here, and the crucifix here; we'll put the refectory in this room and the kitchen there." After a few minutes she had decided precisely what would go where. While walking out she turned to me and said, "Now, Father, give the whole place a good blessing!"

To this day that house is a blessing, providing shelter for mothers in need and for many poor people. Every day, hundreds more needy people go there to get hot soup and a meal. One of the basic principles that Mother Teresa always impressed on us was: "We have to be like tubes." It is not at all important whether these tubes are made of gold, silver or plastic; the important thing is that they let everything through. She once said to her Sisters, "You and I, we are nothing, and in this we see the terrible humility of God. He is so great, so wonderful, that He uses nothingness to show His greatness. And that is why He uses us. Like tubes, we must simply allow God's grace to come through."

This willingness to be "nothing" was an essential part of her. Indeed, she wanted to be just "a pencil in God's hand," a finger pointing toward Jesus. For Mother Teresa, one's own insignificance was the first step toward holiness.

The effect that Mother Teresa had, and still has, on many people is very beautifully illustrated by a story that one of the priests of her congregation told me. Shortly after Mother Teresa received the Nobel Prize, she was welcomed in San Francisco and honored with the symbolic key to the city. The presentation was broadcast by almost all the radio stations in the city. A young man who was heavily involved in drug and weapons dealing was driving along the highway and listening to music on his car radio. When the broadcast of the presentation ceremony began, he searched for a station that had music, but all the stations were broadcasting Mother Teresa's speech. He was frustrated at having to listen to a speech rather than music, but he decided just to wait until the report on the ceremony ended. After listening unwillingly to Mother Teresa for a few minutes, he suddenly began to cry. And he cried so hard that he had to stop the car on the hard shoulder beside the road.

Only when the broadcast was over could he drive on. He called one of the radio stations from the next phone booth to ask who that had been. They told him, "That was Mother Teresa." He looked for, and found, the address of the newly established house of the Sisters in San Francisco and discovered from the Sisters that there was a men's community of the same religious congregation in New York.

So he drove to New York to the Missionaries of Charity Fathers' community and made a retreat there. He made his first confession for many years and began a new life.

14

In the Evil Empire

MOTHER TERESA knew that people are not only hungry for bread; they have another much greater hunger, for dignity, to be loved. "There is not just a thirst for water," she often used to say, "but also a thirst for the Word of God." This hunger and thirst existed both in the Western market-economy countries and also in the Eastern Bloc nations ruled by Communism. They could not be satisfied by either a free market or by Marxist-Leninist or Maoist ideology.

The Eastern Bloc, the great band of atheist states that stretched from the Iron Curtain in the middle of Europe to the Pacific Ocean, ruled by either Moscow or the People's Republic of China, was to a great extent inaccessible at that time to religious communities, and especially to Catholic missionaries. Almost every form of faith and practice was persecuted, even in people's private lives, and was violently suppressed.

The exiled Slovak bishop, Pavol Hnilica, for whom I worked in Rome, had repeatedly asked Mother Teresa to send her Sisters to Russia. He spoke a lot with her about his experiences of Communism. In 1984 he traveled to India with the express purpose of convincing her to send her Sisters to the Soviet Union. At first she hesitated, for she did not want to let her Sisters fall prey to politics. But then she got the approval from

Pope John Paul II—and the papal blessing—for the adventure in the Soviet Union. "You go where I cannot go!" was the Pope's answer. A clear order!

In 1984, on a journey that took me from Calcutta via Moscow to Rome, Mother Teresa had given me a plastic bag full of Miraculous Medals with the request to "plant" them in Moscow. She and her Sisters would storm heaven so that the Mother of God might call the Sisters to Moscow and make it possible for them to establish a foundation in the Soviet Union.

Mother Teresa had already "planted" medals several times for widely varying intentions. For her, I think, it was a special kind of prayer and an act of faith. The medal had to fall into the ground, then you prayed, and then all you had to do was to wait with confidence for the result.

This was a huge thing to ask the Mother of God, for Mother Teresa's congregation of Sisters would be the first Catholic order officially to enter the Communist Soviet Union. And so Mother Teresa gave me a fairly big bag containing several hundred medals to take with me to Moscow.

At that time, one could stay for up to eight days in Moscow with a Soviet travel visa. Bishop Hnilica and I decided to use the maximum allotted time to visit Moscow and to carry out Mother Teresa's assignment. But we had to overcome several difficulties. I still well remember my not entirely optimistic comment about what we could expect from this risky undertaking: "Eight days in Moscow—twenty years in Siberia."

But to tell the story chronologically, first of all we were late getting back to Calcutta from a trip with Mother Teresa to her Sisters' houses in southern India, and so we were forced to postpone our departure to Moscow by a week. However, the Aeroflot travel agency in Calcutta refused to issue new flight tickets because we could not show them the new visas for the rescheduled travel date. At the same time, the Soviet consulate in Calcutta refused to issue us visas until we could show them our changed flight tickets. Both lots of officials remained adamant despite repeated calls. I was near despair and did not know what to do.

Then it occurred to me to take one of the Miraculous Medals that Mother Teresa had given me for Moscow and try it on the lady at the Aeroflot agency in Calcutta. And sure enough, the first little miracle took place. I gave the young lady a medal and said, "I will try one more time to have the visas changed at the consulate, but I really see no hope."

I was at the door, about to leave, when she called me back and said, "Pay attention now. I will paste a sticker with the rescheduled travel date onto your tickets. I am not actually supposed to do that, but that way you can go directly to the consulate. When they give you the visas, remove the sticker immediately and come back here. Then I will officially issue you new tickets." Thus we finally managed to rebook our trip.

In the meantime we had heard that Pope John Paul II, in obedience to Our Lady's request in Fatima, was going to consecrate Russia and the entire world to the Immaculate Heart of Mary on March 25, 1984, the Feast of the Annunciation. The Pope asked all the Catholic bishops to perform this consecration in their own dioceses. But who would do this in the Soviet Union, where there was no Catholic bishop? In Russia, for which the Blessed Mother had intended the act of consecration in a special way?

We flew in our Aeroflot jet via Bangkok to Moscow and arrived in the Soviet capital after midnight. Bishop Hnilica and I were the only passengers who were not taking a connecting flight: instead we planned to use up our travel days in Moscow. So we had to go through customs, which in the Soviet Union was rather strict and unpleasant. They rooted through our luggage and found not only the Bishop's suspicious pectoral cross and several coins from the Vatican, but also the bag with the hundreds of Miraculous Medals. As everyone knew, at that time it was strictly forbidden to bring religious articles into the Soviet Union, and we were ready for major problems. Entering the Soviet Union was by no means risk-free, especially for the exiled Slovak Bishop Hnilica.

Yet here again we saw the miraculous power of the medals. Bishop Hnilica asked the customs official whether he liked the medals and if he wouldn't like to have one. The man looked around quickly, then nodded and took one. We had gotten through customs.

The medal—or the Blessed Mother—worked a similar small miracle a few days later, on March 24, the vigil of the liturgical Feast of the Annunciation, the day on which John Paul II planned to consecrate the world to the Immaculate Heart of Mary. We had "coincidentally" been invited by staff members at an embassy to join a group of diplomats on a tour of the churches in the Kremlin. The official at the entrance objected to a small leather case that the Bishop was carrying in his breast pocket and forbade him to take it along. Once again a medal, a sidelong glance at his policemen colleagues, a nod—and we were in the Kremlin with the leather case in the Bishop's breast pocket, and we were able to visit not only the marvelous Church of St. Michael the Archangel but also the Church of the Annunciation. The contents of the leather case were very important for our plan. We wanted to celebrate Mass—in the middle of the Kremlin, the center of Soviet power—exactly in the church that was dedicated to the mystery of the Annunciation to the Virgin Mary.

Leaning on the throne of the patriarch, the Bishop and I celebrated Holy Mass in the Church of the Annunciation, unnoticed by the numerous tourists. Thanks to its large format the Communist Party newspaper *Pravda* (in English, The Truth) acted as a screen. On the back of the regime's official propaganda sheet, we had no problem hiding the photocopied prayers of the Mass and also the text of the Consecration of the World to the Immaculate Heart of Mary.

After we had performed the consecration, I remembered the assignment that Mother Teresa had given me: to plant medals in the heart of Moscow. The Church of the Annunciation houses the sarcophagi of several tsars. Some of the sarcophagi stood very slightly away from the wall, and my feeling was that a medal dropped into a gap behind a sarcophagus could surely bear fruit for centuries without being disturbed. While no one was looking I threw the medal behind a sarcophagus.

Unfortunately, at that precise moment the general murmuring in the church stopped for a second. The "clink-clink-clink" of the medal hitting the floor could be heard clearly. In a split second, five security guards were on the spot and began agitatedly looking for the cause of the unusual noise. Immediately I had to play the uninterested tourist, though my pulse was definitely racing. After a long, very long, five minutes of unsuccessful searching, the guards gave up. That medal is probably still lying behind the tsar's sarcophagus in the Church of the Annunciation of the Blessed Virgin Mary in the Kremlin. Hopefully it will stay there for the next few centuries.

As a result of Mother Teresa's prayers and faith, that medal has borne much fruit. Today there are more than twenty houses of the Missionaries of Charity in the former Soviet Union.

The following day at six o'clock in the morning we set out on our return trip to Rome. Before leaving the hotel, I gave our names to the sleepy lady at the reception desk to try to settle our account. Her only reply was a gruff *nyet* (no). I repeated our names but again heard only a *nyet*. When the Bishop, who spoke Russian, tried to pay he did not get even a *nyet*. So he simply said, "Well, then we were just guests of the Blessed Mother," and we left the hotel without anyone stopping us.

As luck would have it—because of the two hours' time difference—we landed in Rome at ten the same morning. So it occurred to us that we could perform the "official" Consecration of the World to the Blessed Mother once again, this time together with the Pope at the end of the Solemn High Mass in St. Peter's Square. Although the Roman traffic was so sluggish that I had given up all hope of getting from the airport to the Vatican on time, yet again, things did not turn out as I expected. When we arrived, a Swiss guard led the Bishop and me through the empty basilica, then out through the great main entrance into the dazzling sunlight that enveloped St. Peter's Square on that beautiful Sunday morning. At precisely that moment the Pope began the prayer of the consecration: "Under thy protection we seek refuge, Holy Mother of God. . ."

After the ceremony, Bishop Hnilica gave the Holy Father a report of the secret consecration in the Kremlin and handed him an apple from a market in Moscow—and one of the remaining Miraculous Medals. The Pope was deeply moved by these divine coincidences and saw them as a confirmation from the Blessed Mother that the consecration had been right and in keeping with her request at Fatima.

એ

One year later, in 1985, Mikhail Gorbachev came to power in Moscow, and miracle after miracle began to happen for Mother Teresa, one after the other. The successful establishment of a house with four religious Sisters in the Soviet Union in the 1980's could only be "His work"—in other words, a miracle, pure and simple.

From the start, the legal situation alone—not to mention the political doctrine—seemed to rule out the establishment of a Catholic religious foundation in the Soviet Union. The law prohibited charitable organizations on the territory of the U.S.S.R. When the ideological dogma makes it clear that the State and the Communist Party between them provide everyone with everything they need, what would be the point of a charitable association?

In the Soviet Union, "the Workers' Paradise," there could not possibly be destitute people. That was Communist doctrine.

So the initial response of a high-ranking party official to Mother Teresa's offer to bring her Sisters to Moscow failed: "We have no poor people here in our country. What could your Sisters do here? It is not like in the West; here the state provides people with everything that they need."

Calmly and objectively Mother Teresa replied, "They will bestow tender love and care on those who have no one in their lives. The state cannot do that."

We do not know why, but in 1988 the law forbidding charitable organizations was modified. Thus, for the first time, it became possible to send in the Sisters. This, too, was

"His work"; Mother Teresa was convinced of it. A long series of "preparatory miracles" had been necessary so that her Sisters could lavish "tender love and care" on the poorest of the poor in the Soviet Union.

In July 1987, the two American filmmakers Ann and Jeanette (Jan) Petrie entered their documentary, called *Mother Teresa*, at the Moscow Film Festival. Amid protracted applause from the audience, they won a Soviet Peace Committee prize. Until then, almost no one in the Soviet Union had heard of Mother Teresa, but now everyone was asking, why has this little woman, who has traveled all over the world and accomplished such extraordinary things, never come to the Soviet Union? The answer was simple: She had not yet been invited.

In August 1987, as a result of the award-winning documentary, which may also have touched the hearts of some of the Party leaders, Mother Teresa was awarded the Soviet Peace Committee's Prize for Peace. At that time the president of the Soviet Peace Committee was Genrikh Borovik. Mother Teresa was invited to Moscow for the prize-giving ceremony and she accepted gladly. The necessary visa and travel documents for her "push" into the center of world Communism were prepared in great haste.

Jeanette Petrie, the director of the film, who worked closely with the Sisters, organized the trip. To her horror, Mother Teresa sprang a surprise on her the evening before the flight to Moscow. She would be amazed, said Mother Teresa, at who else was coming on the trip. Jeanette, who was well acquainted with Mother Teresa's determination and drive, was alarmed: "Mother, we certainly won't get a visa for an extra person!"

"This person needs no visa," Mother Teresa grinned and presented a twenty-eight-inch tall statue of the Mother of God to the bewildered group. "She is longing to come with us," Mother Teresa explained. "We have a deal; she helps me to travel to a difficult country and, in exchange, I take her with me. That's how it always works."

Carrying this statue, Mother Teresa arrived in Moscow for the first time ever on August 19, 1987. The prize was presented to her at a solemn ceremony attended by numerous journalists. She was probably very aware that many of the Communist officials intended to make political capital out of her visit. But Mother Teresa never let herself be drawn into political matters.

It was the same this time. In her acceptance speech she addressed her real concern: "I have no silver and gold," she said, quoting the words of Saint Peter to the lame beggar at the Beautiful Gate (Acts 3:6), "but my gift to the peoples of the Soviet Union are my Sisters, whom I am offering." With that she started something that, until then, no one—either inside or outside the Soviet Union—had thought possible: bringing Jesus to Russia's poorest of the poor, right in the heart of Communism, both in the Blessed Sacrament and in loving service from a religious congregation. In view of the persecution of Christians that had begun with Lenin's seizure of power in 1917, and of the ongoing suppression of the faith in what U.S. President Ronald Reagan, not without reason, called "the Evil Empire," that probably really was a miracle.

◌

More than a year passed before the "promised" Sisters got their visas. Then it was time at last; on December 15, 1988, I accompanied Mother Teresa, the newly designated regional superior Sister Mala, Jeanette, and four Sisters to their airplane in Rome to leave for Moscow. There was only one Catholic priest in Moscow, Father Norman, who worked as a diplomat at the French Embassy, so Mother Teresa wanted to bring a priest of their own for the Sisters. I had obtained permission from my bishop in Rome to be at Mother Teresa's disposal if she should need me. To be safe, I had already applied for a visa to the Soviet Union, although I did not expect to be called before the new year.

In addition, during a visit with Mother Teresa to Cardinal Angelo Sodano, the Pope's secretary of state, the Cardinal had already granted me the mandate (required by canon law) that I would need for an assignment in the Soviet Union, including permission to baptize and confirm. I could also "convalidate" Catholic marriages that had been contracted validly though, due to the emergency situation in the Soviet Union, secretly and without a priest. I expected Mother Teresa to call me to Moscow a few days after Christmas, but I already had my visa in my pocket.

Four days before Christmas, I was traveling from Rome via Vienna to Munich to visit my brother and sisters and celebrate Christmas Eve with them. In Vienna a fax reached me from Moscow: "Dear Fr. Leo, come immediately, bring everything. God bless you, Mother Teresa, MC." My family was fairly skeptical when I assured them that I would be back from Moscow in time for Christmas Eve. They proved to be right; I stayed until July.

With two additional Sisters, I boarded the plane to Russia on the evening of that same day. Mother Teresa met us at the airport in Moscow. She was full of enthusiasm and greeted us with the visionary words, "I have asked the Blessed Mother to give us one house in the Soviet Union for each Mystery of the Rosary." (At that time there were fifteen Mysteries of the Rosary, today there are twenty.) Still very much aware of the difficulties that our first group of Sisters, and also I myself, had had obtaining permission to enter at all, I smiled awkwardly. Secretly I thought, somewhat disrespectfully, "Oh dear, she's getting old and starting to imagine things."

Ten years later, on August 25, 1997, two weeks before Mother Teresa's death, I completed a one-week retreat in Moscow for the superiors of all the MC houses in what was, by then, the former Soviet Union. A group picture shows Mother Teresa's incredible visionary power; there were exactly fifteen superiors of the fifteen houses, each with an assistant superior. Each house still bears the name of a Mystery of the Rosary.

ℭ⅌

I knew the Soviet Union from my previous visits, and I also knew the feeling of helplessness that could strike one at a passport checkpoint or hotel entrance when one encountered the seemingly all-powerful policemen or secret service agents. For the cheerful Sisters it must have been a profound shock to be treated imperiously by such people: "Be quiet! Speak only when you are spoken to!"

And *we* were, after all, privileged foreigners. Yet, slowly, but inexorably, I felt a feeling of constriction, indeed of fear, grow within me. It gripped my throat and triggered an instinct to flee. Since the extremely strict checkpoints made any escape from the Soviet Union, the Workers' Paradise, impossible, I felt as though I was in a gigantic, hermetically sealed prison.

This situation, though, had a positive side as well: The prayer "Under thy protection we seek refuge, Holy Mother of God. . ." had suddenly become extremely relevant to us. This prayer, the oldest known prayer to Mary, found on a third-century Egyptian papyrus, inspired me with great trust in God and with the knowledge that the angels and saints are our constant guides and ultimately our only protection.

The drive into the center of Moscow, where the Sisters were being lodged for the time being in three rooms in a hospital, was past endless rows of cold, ugly blocks of residential flats and crowds of people in drab clothing. Their serious, joyless faces hinted at spiritual poverty and unspeakable suffering. The Kremlin, too, and the Lubyanka prison very close by, with its seven stories of basements in which thousands of Christians and opponents of the regime had been tortured and killed, left us deeply disturbed.

Moscow had millions of inhabitants, but only one Catholic church, which we visited. St. Louis stood, significantly, wedged between two buildings belonging to the Soviet Secret Service, the infamous KGB. Everyone knew—and said, though only in secret—that the prisons in the KGB cellars also reached deep under the church.

The Catholic congregation was small and consisted almost entirely of old ladies, known as "babushkas." The atmosphere of fear and mistrust toward every unfamiliar visitor was absolutely tangible. They must still have had lasting memories of how, during the terrible years of the Revolution, secret agents had confiscated the baptismal records of the St. Louis parish and systematically arrested and shot all the Catholics whose names were listed. The very old, almost blind priest celebrated the same Mass every day throughout the year—the Mass for the Dead.

Mother Teresa had an explanation for this grim fact that was both simple and liberating: "He's blind and probably those are the only Mass prayers he knows by heart, the ones from the Mass for the Dead."

In Russia, as in any place where a new house was established, Mother Teresa's first concern was to set up a chapel with the Most Blessed Sacrament. She used one of the three rooms on the seventh floor of the Bolsheviskaya hospital. Jesus' last words on the Cross, "I thirst," are written on the wall in every chapel of the Missionaries of Charity, beneath the right arm of the Crucified Christ. They explain why Mother Teresa wanted to bring her Sisters to the very center of atheism: God's loving desire, His "thirst" to love and to be loved, is limited neither by political nor by cultural or governmental boundaries.

Then came Christmas Eve. In the midst of the spiritual poverty of that city, and surrounded by the suffering people of the huge Bolsheviskaya hospital, the little group surrounding Mother Teresa celebrated Mass at midnight. It was not just the height of the seventh floor that made heaven seem near: the birth of Christ was being celebrated, with official permission, by a small group of Catholic missionary Sisters in the heart of the Soviet Union for the first time since the October Revolution in 1917—a tiny grain of wheat that was to produce much fruit.

The news that a Mass would be celebrated that evening in the hospital had spread like wildfire among the nurses, doctors and patients. Despite the general anti-religious atmosphere and the risk they were taking, the hospital-room chapel was bursting with its first visitors. At the end, they left as silently as they had come.

15

Soviet Christmas

THE SOVIET UNION was a permanent "sea of misery." Tragically, the misery became even worse when, in the second week of December 1988, there was a major earthquake in Armenia so strong that it collapsed whole multistory buildings like houses of cards. The regions around Spitak and Leninakan (now called Gjumri) were especially hard hit. There were more than thirty thousand deaths, among them thousands of children.

The Sisters had not even finished moving into their house in Moscow when Mother Teresa accepted the invitation from a representative of the Armenian Peace Committee to send four Sisters, along with a priest, to Yerevan, the capital of Armenia. They were to offer "humble love and service" at a children's hospital and thereby give the children and their families comfort and hope at this very difficult time. The hospital had been built a few years earlier for 120 children; now, however, it was occupied by more than 600, for the most part victims of the earthquake.

Our quick, indeed rushed, departure from Moscow gave us scarcely any time to prepare. "Wait and see" was not Mother Teresa's motto, nor was it her policy on this occasion. Christmas, the celebration of Jesus' birth, was, in her view, precisely the right day to make haste to help the stricken population of Armenia with four nuns—and a priest. The flight from Moscow to Yerevan was therefore immediately scheduled for the afternoon of Christmas Day. Neither our wordless amazement at the haste nor a raging snowstorm could delay our journey, at least as far as Moscow's Sheremetyevo International Airport.

Since not only Moscow but also our destination, Yerevan, was in danger of being submerged by snow, we had to wait at Sheremetyevo for hours. Since we were with Mother Teresa, who was still being treated as an honorary guest of the Soviet Peace Committee, we were VIPs and had the privilege of spending the time in a special airport lounge for Party and KGB members. This room was reserved for high-ranking Party and industry bosses. Its normally heavy and silent atmosphere of power, or perhaps of fear, could not have been more strikingly transformed by the lively, excited chatter of the young, coffee-brown Indian Sisters in their radiant white-and-blue saris.

Indian saris and a Moscow blizzard, ice-cold wind at temperatures below freezing, and Mother Teresa in her open-toed leather sandals and no socks—what could more clearly symbolize the contrast between Communist power and evangelical poverty? Even the concrete KGB lounge, with its overblown, tasteless plastic furniture and astonishingly uncared-for wall-to-wall carpeting, was changed in a way which no one there would ever have expected.

When waiting was unavoidable, Mother Teresa always filled the time with prayer, apostolic work, and cheerful conversation and laughter with her Sisters. So, too, on that Christmas Day, the guests waiting in the VIP lounge were greeted warmly. Even a tentative, shy smile was rewarded with a Miraculous Medal from Mother Teresa's bag of treasures. She and her Sisters took every sign of curiosity, every questioning glance, as a welcome opportunity to bestow a smile or a friendly word. Soon all the guests had the Bogoroditsa (Mother of God)—Mother Teresa was already using the Russian word—in the form of a Miraculous Medal hanging on a chain or a string around their necks, or stowed away in their briefcases. She taught those who spoke a little English a prayer to go with the medal: "Mary, Mother of Jesus, be Mother to me."

The guests' joy and amazement at these little gestures of love were great. And great, too, was the general amazement when the armchairs were pushed together and the Sisters quietly, out of consideration for those present, prayed and sang their midday prayers in that VIP lounge reserved for the Soviet ruling class. There was a silence throughout that large room that would have been fitting during prayers in a cathedral on Christmas Eve. My only fear was that the guards in front of the door would suddenly put an end to these devotions taking place in the heart of the Soviet Empire and restore atheist "normality."

But nothing of the sort happened. Scarcely had the final Hail Mary faded away when the Sisters opened their bags and boxes and magically produced fresh Moscow black bread, soft cheese and—read it and marvel!—little chocolate Easter eggs. Easter eggs on Christmas Day!

All the passengers were invited to share the sandwiches and Easter eggs, though only the bravest accepted the plastic cups of fizzy, yellow-green liquid that one of the Sisters produced from her bag. After a cheerful half hour, the leftovers were packed away and the plastic cups washed; it was time for a well-earned rest. Mother Teresa sat down in a pseudo-Baroque armchair beneath a huge painting, took out a newspaper and began deciphering the Cyrillic letters that she must have learned as a child at the Serbian school in Skopje. Soon she nodded off. The newspaper almost completely covered her. I shall never forget the sight of Mother Teresa on Christmas Day 1988, in Moscow, at the heart of the Soviet Empire, sitting on a Baroque throne beneath a giant picture of Lenin, with the Communist Party newspaper *Pravda* spread over her. She slept completely peacefully.

❧

Out on the airfield, the big white snowflakes continued to fall furiously for hours. A flight out of Moscow was unthinkable until the evening. Eventually, however, when it was already dark, our plane took off, although lots of other flights had been canceled. Until the last minute it was extremely uncertain whether we would be able to land at the airport in Yerevan, since this had also been damaged by the earthquake. Even though it was several days since the devastating quake, relief and military aircraft bringing in vital supplies and search parties for the victims still had priority over civilian aircraft. After a series of Mother Teresa's beloved Quick Novenas we finally landed in the middle of a snowstorm. The pilot executed an approach that resembled the various stages of a roller-coaster ride; the airplane lurched and groaned terrifyingly.

For a moment I thought it would surely be comforting to die beside Mother Teresa. But then another, even stronger feeling took over, which other people with Mother Teresa in different crises have also experienced. In her presence, there was seldom fear or panic. It was as though the Hand that so obviously guided, carried and enfolded Mother Teresa would also hold and protect us, as long as we were near her.

Having landed in Yerevan, we did not have long to wait for the next crisis. It was shortly after midnight and we had just left the main hall of the airport, when all the lights were turned out and the doors were locked behind us. Our arrival after the long delay had evidently not been expected—or at least no one had come to meet us.

So we stood on the street in the dark, on that Christmas night, in a blizzard, alone and freezing cold. Yerevan was two miles away. This time, instead of a Quick Novena, Mother Teresa began to pray the Third Joyful Mystery of the Rosary, the Nativity of Our Lord in Bethlehem, with us. We had not yet finished the ten Hail Marys when Mother Teresa pointed out to us—with a loud "See how good Jesus is!"—that God had once again helped her and us, this time in the form of a large police van whose headlights suddenly appeared out of the dense blizzard.

From its size, I concluded that this van was intended to transport troops or convey prisoners. And I would hardly have blamed the police officers if they had taken these midnight wanderers, clad in exotic saris and sandals on the snow-covered airport road, directly to a locked institution. Instead, they drove us into the capital and dropped us off, as they had clearly been instructed, in front of the children's hospital; for the next several months this was to be the Sisters' new home and mine.

Apparently the police had also informed the hospital administration that we had, after all, appeared, despite the inclement weather—a large delegation was awaiting us at the entrance to the hospital. It consisted of the director and several doctors (all female) and a few other ladies—apparently all friends of the director—and the security personnel, whom I, in my mind, immediately classified as KGB agents; everyone was very keen to give us the impression that they had prepared everything for our arrival.

As soon as they had shown us around, Mother Teresa set about dividing up the rooms, making lighthearted comments, but at the same time appearing very determined. We did not have much space. The hospital had originally been designed for 120 children. Now, after the earthquake, there were more than 600, some of them severely injured. They lay along the corridors and in the stairwells.

Two rooms had been provided for the four Sisters whom Mother Teresa had brought with her. Without pausing for a moment, Mother Teresa began to set up a chapel in one of them; she unpacked a crucifix that she had brought along and a small portable tabernacle. A few minutes later the crucifix was hanging on the wall with the inscription "I thirst," a table had been brought in as an altar, and a mat had been unrolled on the floor. The Sisters were already able to say their first prayers of thanksgiving and their night prayers.

On another part of the same floor, Mother Teresa found for me a tiny dark storage room of about seventy-five square feet, with only a small high window opening onto an office. I must have looked into the room with some surprise, perhaps even horror. Mother Teresa, who had already inspected it, declared, "Now, Father, you really are a missionary!" There was an unmissable undertone of satisfied triumph in her words.

Then she pulled a little package of dried prunes from her patched "horn of plenty" bag, gave me a prune, and said, "Good night!" And there I was, standing with a prune in my hand in that tiny room that was almost filled by the "bed," a wooden frame and two sacks of straw sewn together to make a mattress.

How could I possibly fit anything in here? I had nothing anyway, absolutely nothing but the clothes I was wearing. My luggage had gone missing on the flight from Rome to Moscow and was never seen again. I consoled myself with the thought that this accommodation was only for one night.

My Armenian adventure had begun. On that strange Christmas night in faraway Yerevan I devoured my sumptuous dinner, the prune that Mother Teresa had handed me. I was about to spit out the pit. But wait! Don't waste anything! Could there perhaps still be some use for the pit? And there was: for the next two weeks, for want of an alternative, that was my toothbrush.

Exhausted, I slept soundly for the few hours until morning Mass. No doubt I would not have slept so well had I known that this "sleeping compartment with small high window" was to be not just an emergency solution for one night, but my lodging for the next five months.

16

Armenian Adventure

THE ACCOMMODATION and living conditions over the next weeks, which eventually turned into months, were the worst I have ever experienced. There was no electricity and therefore no light in my room, since it had no outside window but only the inner window into the office next door. There was no washbasin in my room and, of course, no hot water in the shared washroom nearby. And yet, looking back, I can say that those were the most wonderful months of my life.

This was probably because of the "official instructions" that Mother Teresa gave us the very next morning after Holy Mass: "What did we come here for? We came to proclaim Christ in the poorest of the poor by giving humble love and service and do that with a smile."

That same morning I was privileged to witness a scene that showed me what "humble love and service" meant in practice. I was coming out of my room and was about to turn the corner to the staircase when I saw a group of people standing at the top of the staircase. They had stopped and were all watching something with obvious fascination. Only after about three minutes did they start moving again. Then I saw the reason for their fascination—Mother Teresa and two of her Sisters, bent double, were scrubbing the floor with cloths.

Although the hospital had been open and running for three years, the toilets and the long corridors and staircases had never been cleaned—not once! Under Mother Teresa's direction and with her help, the Sisters had, without many words, immediately turned the "official instructions" into a "living action," as Mother Teresa often taught. All the washing and toilet facilities and corridors were systematically cleaned, one by one, over the next few weeks, starting on the top floor.

At the same time, the injured and traumatized children were being caressed, supplied with Miraculous Medals, and washed. The Sisters supported the hospital staff wherever and whenever possible and gave encouragement to the nurses. Indeed, encouragement was urgently needed, since the doctors and nurses were hopelessly overwhelmed by the constant influx of new arrivals, mainly seriously injured children.

The earthquake, just before Christmas, had taken the lives of more than thirty thousand people in Armenia, in the region where most of the few Catholics in Armenia lived. For more than sixty years many of them had preserved their faith, often secretly and in the most difficult circumstances. Now the children's hospital in Yerevan was hopelessly overcrowded. What God's plan was in all this, we will probably only learn in eternity.

သာ

On December 28, 1988, Mother Teresa signed an agreement with the local Peace Committee, a Soviet governmental organization that was in charge of monitoring all foreigners who were not just tourists. Mother Teresa promised that she—or more precisely, I—would only serve the Sisters within the hospital, would hold no public conferences or religious celebrations outside the hospital, and would cause no political disturbances. Naturally it was impossible for me to keep all those promises; as a priest I could not only concern myself with the souls of the four Sisters.

Whenever one of the children was dying, the young women doctors working directly above me in the intensive care unit would signal by knocking on the floor three times with the heels of their shoes. I would hurry upstairs to the first floor and they would give me the necessary information, for instance 18-C. Then I would know that the third child in the eighteenth row was near to death, and I could do my priestly duty. Thus I baptized many children in the final moments of their lives. This involved no little risk, as was clear from the example of a Polish priest who had come to Armenia as a relief worker and had baptized a child at the request of its parents. The authorities learned about this and expelled him the very next day.

In several cases I had to ask myself under what circumstances I could administer baptism to an unbaptized adult who was about to die. I remembered Mother Teresa explaining to me that a dying person does not have to know the entire teaching of the Catholic Church in order for us to be able to baptize him. At the moment of death, it is enough for the dying person to grasp the core of the Church's teaching, namely, the love of God. One only needed to ask the dying person if he "would like to go to the God who sent the Sisters to him." A wonderful question, to which probably no one privileged to experience God's love through those loving hands could answer no.

The Sisters' loving care had such a fantastic effect on the children's recovery that almost inexplicable cures took place. One of Mother Teresa's Sisters had, in my opinion, a very special gift of healing. When she prayed for children, laid her hands on them and blessed them, an astonishing number recovered very quickly. We saw this with a little girl who had a degenerative condition that affected her limbs and airways so that she was becoming increasingly paralyzed. When the doctors concluded that she was likely to die before the night was over, I heard the triple knock again, went upstairs and baptized her. The Sister was with me and prayed for the little girl. We were both sure that I would have to bless the child's dead body the next day. But the following day, her lungs were no longer paralyzed and she could breathe freely again. Three weeks later, she came to the Sisters in the chapel to do a dance for them in thanksgiving for their prayers. This cure was so extraordinary that the doctors reported it to the director of the hospital—and she in turn reported it to the Armenian Medical Association. Then the "case of this inexplicable cure" was included in a report to the health authorities in the all-controlling Moscow bureaucracy.

Moscow promptly sent an official delegation of doctors and psychiatrists to Yerevan with instructions to find out what "healing method" Mother Teresa's Sisters used. We were questioned by three physicians and psychologists, among them a very young intern, for an entire afternoon. The Sisters showed them the Miraculous Medal and explained how to pray. Considering the state's strictly materialistic ideology, it was quite astounding that the investigating commission seemed to be satisfied with this explanation. They took the

Miraculous Medal, taped it to one of the pages of their report, and traveled contentedly back to Moscow.

Two years later I was standing on a street corner in Moscow when suddenly I heard a man calling from across the street, "Father Leo, Father Leo!" I looked and recognized the former intern from the investigating commission.

"Father, what an extraordinary coincidence that I should meet you right now," he greeted me. "I was baptized yesterday in the Orthodox Church. That may well be another effect of the Miraculous Medal that you gave us."

ආ

The "Peace Committee" was a high-ranking government authority; I believed it was entirely made up of Party members and KGB agents. Whether or not that was so, the authorities in Yerevan, from the police to the hospital director, always followed the orders of Peace Committee members.

Mother Teresa clearly recognized that this organization could provide the best protection for the Sisters and me; in a very short time she had even made special friends in the committee, both in Moscow and in Yerevan. These were mostly women whose hearts she had touched with a few words and a Miraculous Medal, and to whom she had showed something entirely new: "God loves you! He has written you in the palm of His hand. You are His! He created you to love and to be loved."

Mother Teresa had taken many of these women to her heart. She was shocked when she learned about the plight of her new friends, about their failed marriages and their many abortions, which were routine practice in the Soviet Union. "Poor child," she often said, without any reproach, almost as though she herself was painfully wounded and immediately ready to comfort—but she also told them clearly about the path to a new life based on the principle "to love and to be loved."

"God loves the world through us," Mother Teresa used to say. And she was always the first to put this into practice. Even years later—at a time when, from a political point of view, the Sisters no longer needed this kind of protection—Natasha, a secretary of the committee, or other friends she had made would receive a short letter or a holiday postcard from Mother Teresa. She sent these letters and cards from all over the world and always added a few words expressing genuine gratitude. Thanks to her almost photographic memory, she always remembered the people who had helped her.

When Mother Teresa signed the agreement with the local Peace Committee at the end of December, my suspicion became a certainty. My stay in the beautiful Armenian Soviet Socialist Republic was not just a Christmas excursion, as I had assumed. Mother Teresa wanted to make "a real missionary" out of me. God's plan seemed to be on her side.

The agreement that Mother Teresa had signed stipulated that the priest whose presence had been a prerequisite for the Sisters to come to Armenia would not make public appearances but was there only for the Sisters. But now, every day, hundreds of people would invite the Sisters to their homes. This was part of the very strong Armenian tradition of hospitality. But, as mentioned earlier, under the constitution of the Missionaries of Charity, the Sisters are not allowed to eat outside their houses.

Mother Teresa had introduced this rule in Calcutta so that the poor would not have to share the little that they have with the Sisters; hospitality in India demands that guests always come first. You always share with guests whatever you have. Mother Teresa established this general rule that the Sisters are never allowed to eat outside their own houses, in order to make sure that the Sisters would not involuntarily take back from the poor what they had just given them. Since she herself followed this rule with an iron will, the poor quickly accepted the fact that the Sisters did not eat in their homes—not out of discourtesy but simply because that is their rule.

In Armenia this rule presented us with new challenges. Mother Teresa managed to resolve the dilemma without offending Armenian hospitality and, at the same time, without deviating from her own rule—she assigned to me the task of accepting the countless invitations in place of the Sisters. Because I was not bound by their constitution, I had to attend a dinner almost every day during those six months in Armenia. This was, among other things, an arduous test of my health, for protocol demanded that first the master of the house should give a speech, then the guest, and then usually the oldest son of the household as well. And after each speech, everyone had to drink a large glassful of excellent Armenian cognac.

Sometimes friends and friends of friends came to these meals, so the number of guests present might be forty or fifty. That was already risky, because Mother Teresa had agreed in writing that I would perform no public actions outside the hospital and also would not preach. In reality, however, these evenings were pure catechism instruction. Every evening, people would ask me lots of questions about the Christian faith. Their interest was immense. Often someone would say, "I was baptized a Catholic." So as not to draw the attention of the Soviet authorities to our meetings—which would have endangered the guests themselves as well as the Sisters—I soon asked that no more than twenty people be invited on any evening.

At that time the Soviet army had declared a curfew in Yerevan. Everybody had to be home by ten in the evening. Anyone found on the street even one minute after ten was arrested and locked up overnight in the local stadium. At twenty degrees Celsius below zero (well below freezing), that must have been very unpleasant. Those who had been locked up were always tried at dawn the next day. At ten o'clock every evening, Soviet tanks drove up the major access roads to Yerevan and blocked them all with heavy chains. Later, in the summer months, the curfew generally began at eleven.

For me the curfews were indirectly helpful; they gave me an unarguable reason to leave these dinners, with their rich food and heavy drinking, before ten o'clock. Otherwise I certainly would never have made it back by five the next morning to celebrate morning prayers and Holy Mass with the Sisters.

When summer came, the Sisters considered setting up a house for themselves in Spitak, with the help of the Italian Protezione Civile (Civil Guard), in the center of the area that had been devastated by the earthquake, so that they could care for the people there on the spot. I frequently had to drive about seventy miles north to Spitak and often got back late in the evening. At this time the curfew was set at 11:00 P.M. On one occasion I was driving back in a car with a blue lamp that had been placed at my disposal by the Protezione Civile; it was relatively late and so I was driving fast. On the final stretch of the highway before the city, the speed limit was reduced to twenty miles per hour so that the police could identify everyone as they drove past. I was annoyed by this nonsense and sped along at eighty miles per hour: I also had to be back before eleven because of the curfew.

I was driving much too fast as I reached the bridge into town. I saw the heavy Soviet tanks already in position. I decided to drive between them at high speed; in the poor light I only noticed at the last minute that the eight-inch chain was already stretched between them, blocking the bridge. Tires squealing, I braked. My car came to a stop up against the chain.

My heart was pounding. What would the Soviet soldiers do now? By my clock it was still a few seconds before eleven. The soldiers came running agitatedly. They saw the blue lamp on my car roof and my clerical collar. Aha, that foreigner again!—they may have thought. I greeted them friendlily and tried Mother Teresa's method: "I have a present for you here!" I pressed a Miraculous Medal into the hand of each soldier. No miracle, but still success—the soldiers took down the chain and I was able to drive home in peace rather than spending the night in the stadium.

ↄ

The thing that the Armenians are proudest of, and at the same time their greatest sorrow, is the emblem of their country— Mount Ararat. It is, in fact, a huge group of mountains that rises so evenly in a classic volcano shape that you hardly notice how high it really is from the observation point and tourist attraction in Armenia about two miles south of Yerevan. This view is so painful for Armenians because their emblem is situated not in Armenian but in Turkish territory. Since the end of World War I they have been separated from their emblem by a national border.

On the terrace leading up to the observation platform sat an old woman with crippled legs. The Sisters' attention was focused not so much on the beautiful mountain as on this Armenian (as we thought) beggar woman with her disheveled, matted hair. She was sitting on the stone floor in the sun—though its warmth was scarcely perceptible in the icy cold—in torn, horribly filthy rags. She was clearly incapable of moving by herself.

The woman declined the Sisters' invitation that we take her with us immediately. She said she had someone who brought her there to beg and then took her back home again. We learned later that the man who transported her received two-thirds of the proceeds of her begging for his services. Begging was forbidden under Soviet law, which is why aiding and abetting this "crime" had its price. Mother Teresa and our translator Anahit promised Irna (for that was her name) a visit from the Sisters at her home within the next few days.

Several days later we went to Irna's "home," carrying blankets, food and cleaning supplies. Even at a distance we could see that it was a ramshackle shed meant for hay or fodder, almost flattened by the wind, on the edge of a large field that had been planted with crops. Inside the shed it stank so horribly that I was grateful to be able to take on the job of fetching water. Since Irna could not move, her room had clearly not been cleaned for years and was indescribably filthy. Everything was sticky and covered with a layer of dust and grime. The things that she used stood within reach around her bed—that is, around the three sacks of straw on the broken bed frame on which she slept. A little gas burner served as both a heater and a cooker. About three layers of cracked, unwashed glasses stood above that flame, and the highest glass, which was not yet broken, contained the remnants of a grayish-brown liquid. The Sisters, the translator and I worked the whole day. Under Irna's bed we found the bones of two fish and a dead rat.

It was already evening, and we were packing up all the garbage that we had cleared out in order to cart it away, when Anahit had the idea of asking Irna whether she would like to make her confession to me.

I was clearly not yet a "real missionary" because at first I saw all sorts of reasons against hearing such a confession: Irna was surely of the Armenian Orthodox faith, and besides that I did not understand her language. Anahit reminded me, however, that a confession via an interpreter is definitely permitted and said that she was willing to interpret. Mother Teresa's words encouraged me: "Father, be a real missionary!"

So I went back again into the room, which still stank incredibly. "Yes, I would like to make confession," said Irna, beaming and suddenly beginning in broken English with the Sign of the Cross! Her very first words hit me like a slap from God on the back of the head: "I am Catholic." After her confession, when I had given her absolution, Irna told me her life story. In her youth she had been a Catholic nun. At the age of eighteen she had entered a convent in Syria. Her parents were opposed to her decision, and after a few years they forced her to leave the convent and marry. She moved to Armenia with her husband. When her two sons were grown up they returned with their father to Syria and she remained alone in Armenia.

For twenty years she had heard nothing from her husband and children. Since then her life had consisted of begging and prayer. Every day she had prayed to God to forgive her for leaving the convent, and to grant her the grace to live long enough to make a Catholic confession and receive Holy Communion again one last time.

Now I understood why her eyes had shone at the moment of absolution. They had transformed that sorry room into a little paradise. No poverty, no stench—the mystery of God's incomprehensible Providence and love was so close that you could grasp it.

Three weeks later I spoke with Mother Teresa on the telephone. "How is Irna?" was her very first question. "God called her back home to Himself," I answered. "She died with a radiant smile."

Mother Teresa's response, "Do you understand now what a real missionary is?" reminded me of my mission and of the fact that we are, as she liked to say, only "pencils in God's hand."

જી

During those months in Armenia we very often touched the poorest of the poor. We were not always able to help them a great deal, but we always touched them with our love and care—sometimes only to console them, sometimes to be with them when they died. When I look back, I recall that I was nearly in tears when I left Yerevan. It was certainly the toughest time of my life, but it was also the most beautiful, the time when I probably encountered Jesus most frequently and was most often able to quench His thirst.

Through her Sisters and through her own example, Mother Teresa helped me to experience Jesus' presence. And that half year in Armenia was an outstanding education for me— I learned a great deal about human capabilities and qualities and also an object lesson in how grace works. At the end of those six months I realized that the Sisters had not quarreled once with each other or with me. And yet all four had very different and in some cases very forceful characters. There was a complete unity and harmony between them, although it was materially and also psychologically an extremely difficult time. At the end I felt as though I was being driven out of a paradise.

Mother Teresa would surely say, "Father, you don't need to travel to Armenia at all to discover Jesus," just as she often said, "You don't need to come to Calcutta at all to discover Jesus in the poorest of the poor. The poor are right there where you are, very often in your own families. Look for them, find them and put your love for Jesus into a living action for them."

17

With Pilgrims, Prostitutes and Politicians

MOTHER TERESA advised many of her visitors to Calcutta from Western Europe and America to care for the needy and the poor in their own countries. During her travels she had become well aware that there were the poorest of the poor also living in the shadow of prosperity. That is why she called the long bridge in New York City that connects Manhattan with the Bronx "Reality Bridge," "because you change from one reality to another reality" in crossing it—from wealthy Manhattan with its skyscrapers and grand hotels to the impoverished Bronx with the slums of New York.

In the summer of 1986, the Communauté de l'Emmanuel (the Emmanuel Community) invited Mother Teresa to their center in Paray-le-Monial (in Burgundy in eastern France) for a large family conference. Here, Saint Margaret-Mary Alacoque (1647–1690) saw her visions of the Sacred Heart of Jesus. After some thought, Mother Teresa agreed to go and decided to combine it with a trip to Paris. Presumably, as well as her own devotion to the Sacred Heart, which had begun in her childhood, there were two practical reasons for making this journey in July 1986. One was that the Sisters in Paris urgently needed a bigger house for their poor people. She hoped to get help with obtaining a house from Bernadette Chirac, the wife of the newly installed French prime minister and long-time mayor of Paris, Jacques Chirac. Madame Chirac, a practicing Catholic, was well disposed toward the Sisters.

After landing in Paris, we went by high-speed train to Paray-le-Monial. It was always a great joy for the Missionaries of Charity to see Mother Teresa personally because the Sisters living in Europe very seldom had that joy.

I remember their joy at the privilege of meeting with Mother Teresa and hearing the stirring speech that she gave to the two thousand families. Her central message was very simple: "The family that prays together, stays together." I learned, to my relief, that I did not have to translate Mother Teresa's talk because the Dominican priest Albert-Marie de Monléon—who today is bishop of Meaux—took on the job of interpreting. Although there were naturally a lot of children at this family congress, the room was very quiet as Mother Teresa began her speech.

I marveled at the beautiful translation by Père Albert. He turned Mother Teresa's simple language into simple but very cultivated French. I have rarely heard such a good translation. I was all the more astonished afterward when Père Albert came to me and said, "That was a really wonderful talk but I'm very upset that I could only manage such a miserable translation. I really couldn't express everything that Mother Teresa put into her words."

His remark was an important consolation for me, because I had exactly that feeling myself. Whenever I translated for Mother Teresa, I never managed to do it accurately. It always seemed that a lot got lost in the translation. I once had to translate a speech she gave in Vienna and I remember thinking, "Oh, terrible! That was really a thoroughly miserable translation."

But then an American who had lived in Vienna for thirty years came and said, "Father Leo, what a fantastic translation!"

I am convinced that a translator must simply do his best— and the Holy Spirit does all the rest. I have often thought if I myself were to say the things that Mother Teresa was saying and I am translating, but without her standing beside me, it would be nothing at all. Her personality and her holiness have an effect simply because she is there, because the idea or the word comes from her, even though it reaches the listener through my translation. That is what people experienced— not the mere words, but the sanctity of the person from whom those words came.

That evening it was back to Paris, where we arrived very late. The Sisters' house was not far from a red light district where the following incident is said to have taken place. Mother Teresa was driving toward the Sisters' house. On the street corner some "ladies of the night" were standing. Suddenly Mother Teresa told the driver to stop. She rolled down the window and said to one of the ladies, "Come to our house; it's straight ahead, not far from here." The next day the woman came to the house. Today, the story goes, she is a Catholic nun.

&

One day we heard that the new prime minister, Jacques Chirac, who only had been in office for a few weeks, would receive us in his official chambers at ten o'clock that same morning. After morning Mass and breakfast we set out for the Hotel Matignon, the prime minister's official residence. Monsieur Chirac had been mayor of Paris since 1977 and had led the opposition against the Socialist president Mitterand. But the results of the most recent election had forced Monsieur Mitterand to collaborate with Monsieur Chirac, his greatest challenger (who became president himself in 1995). We drove along the Rue de Bac, the street on which the Church of Saint Catherine Laboure stands. Her visions of the Blessed Virgin Mary are the origin of the Miraculous Medal and, when Mother Teresa learned this, she immediately wanted to stop there to pray.

Mother Teresa always had her "ammunition"—the Miraculous Medals—with her in whichever bag she was carrying. She seemed to have a very personal relationship with the Mother of God, and she wanted to extend this relationship to other people through the Miraculous Medals. So we went into the church and prayed. As soon as the Sisters of the congregation living there heard that Mother Teresa was in the church, they all came running, and the general superior greeted Mother Teresa very warmly.

The conversation quickly turned to the fact that Mother Teresa distributed a lot of medals herself; indeed, you could say that this was her most important "pastoral tool." Everyone she met received a medal from her. Usually she kissed the medal and briefly showed the person how to wear it round his or her neck. Sometimes she added the explanation that we can always trust the Mother of God, for she protects us, miraculously if necessary. So Mother Teresa told the general superior that she had distributed enormous quantities of medals with her own hands.

The general superior said, "That's wonderful! May we perhaps give you a few medals, so you don't have to buy them?"

"Yes, please."

"How many do you need, five hundred or one thousand?"

Mother Teresa replied, "Forty thousand! That is how many I have already distributed."

I do not think we were given forty thousand medals, but we stowed as many boxes as possible in the trunk of the car before we left.

༃

On we went to the Hotel Matignon. We were very impressed by the palace's grandeur and beauty. In the first great reception hall there was an enormous glass table, about thirteen feet by twenty-six feet, on the right. The tabletop was made of two layers of glass. Between the layers there were leaves—all made of gold—that looked as though they had just blown in, in an artistic way. This must have been a masterpiece by some French artist, but I could not help thinking of the foil in which chocolates are wrapped. Mother Teresa evidently had very similar associations. She looked for a moment at the table and said, "Hmm, they must have eaten lots of chocolate."

Then we went up the stairs to the prime minister's reception room. Monsieur Chirac walked quickly over to greet us and a conversation developed between him and Mother Teresa. Still completely filled with the beautiful liturgy she had experienced with the Emmanuel Community, she asked Monsieur Chirac, "Have you ever been to Paray-le-Monial?"

He was surprised. "Not yet."

"You must go. You must go!"

The prime minister tried to remain polite and said, "Yes, yes."

Mother Teresa insisted, "Yes, will you travel there? Will you?"

Chirac tried to avoid the question: "Well, anyway. . ."

But Mother Teresa simply would not let go. "Yes? When will you go there? But only you alone. Only you and Jesus, all alone! Not in a crowd. You and Jesus."

Monsieur Chirac did not say no immediately, and Mother Teresa saw this as her opportunity. "Then go!" Turning to

Francis Kohn from the Communauté de l'Emmanuel, she added: "Father, you organize the trip for . . . you organize the trip for. . . ."

Then she asked Father Kohn quietly, "Who is he?"

He leaned over to her and said, "The prime minister!"

Mother Teresa said out loud, "Well, good; then you can organize the trip for Mr. Prime Minister!"

Later it was reported that Monsieur Chirac did in fact go to Paray-le-Monial—not alone with Jesus, however, but with a large entourage. Evidently Mother Teresa's suggestion had had some effect on him. However, she was less successful with obtaining the house for the poor than she had hoped for. It took many more months before the Sisters got a new house.

18

Among Hindus and Muslims

WHEN MOTHER TERESA picked a human being out of the gutter, when she gave the poor something to eat or bestowed attention and tender love on the dying, she never made a distinction with regard to religious affiliation. Hindus and Muslims, Christians and people without God, could all count just the same on her love and care.

The reason for this lies in the inner logic of Christianity: What sort of Christians would they be who only acted in a Christian way toward Christians? But for Mother Teresa there was an even deeper reason: In every poor, suffering, needy or dying person whom she took in, she saw Jesus, hidden in the distressing disguise of the poorest of the poor.

Every day in Calcutta she mainly encountered Hindus, but also Muslims. These encounters shaped her relationship with other religions. Again and again, she used to say that every human being can come closer to God if he practices his own religion well and seeks the truth with sincerity of heart. And if a person wants to come closer to God, then God can also do something with him and lead him further. Mother Teresa would say, "Doesn't matter race, doesn't matter religion, Christian or Communist doesn't matter—we are all created to love and be loved."

Respecting the beliefs of other people does not, however, mean ignoring their religious affiliation as though it were insignificant. Quite the contrary: When a person was brought to Mother Teresa's House for the Dying, the Sisters immediately asked his name and religion—if he was still capable of speech. That was not a form of discrimination; each person's religion was noted so that the Sisters would know which ritual to use for the funeral.

The Missionaries of Charity see to it that everyone who dies in their care is buried or cremated according to the rites of his own religion. And because no one who dies there has any money, the Sisters also pay for it.

Once, when Bishop Hnilica was living with the Jesuits, he returned late and found the doors locked; he asked Mother Teresa whether he could spend the night at her House for the Dying, Nirmal Hriday (House of the Pure Heart). Mother Teresa reflected for a moment and then agreed, but on one condition: "Promise me you won't die. The burial of a bishop would be much too expensive for us."

❦

Mother Teresa's knowledge of other religions, especially Hinduism and Islam, was not mainly theological; it concentrated more on the practical matters of life: customary fasts and feast days, dietary and burial regulations, morality. Mother Teresa was no theorist: "We see the needs and we act." When I asked her once about the causes of poverty in Africa, she told me, "You see, Father, we don't think about this sort of question. We don't think about the why, how and when. We simply see the need—and help as well as we can."

When she did investigate causes, she did so from a spiritual perspective as in the following incident. During a long car journey, Mother Teresa suddenly asked, "How could Communism ever come about?" Bishop Hnilica, who was a seasoned expert in questions of Communist ideology, which he had experienced personally, tried to present the historical reasons. Mother Teresa did not seem satisfied. Her concern was to understand how such an invasion into the Mystical Body of Christ, into the structure of the Church, was possible.

She was almost shy in presenting her version: "Why was it possible for Judas to betray our Lord? He was so close to Jesus, and Jesus loved him so much! I think that it happened because he was a thief, because he stole money from the poor. I think that that was the reason." I have often reflected on this explanation of a worldwide tragedy like Communism, and I think that this way of contemplating the world is still valid today. Whenever the poor are "robbed," whenever they are deprived of their right to a life of human dignity, the social order—and the order of love for one another in the broader sense—is severely wounded.

ᜃ

Setting up accommodation for the dying, and in a house that was formerly for pilgrims to the Kali Temple in Calcutta, was anything but easy and straightforward. Radical Hindu groups feared a Christian missionary campaign and accused the Sisters of proselytizing and of recruiting from among the Hindu faithful. There were violent protests when the Calcutta authorities granted Mother Teresa the use of these premises.

At that time a distinguished Hindu leader came from Delhi to enlist the local youth in driving Mother Teresa and her Sisters out of the precincts of the Kali Temple. Armed with cudgels and stones, the mob approached, with the Hindu leader in the forefront. When Mother Teresa heard what was happening, she stood in front of the door and then walked toward the mob. She greeted the leader without any sign of fear and invited him to come in and see what they were doing.

He went in with her by himself. After a while he came out again. The youths crowded around and asked him whether they could now begin to drive out the Sisters. He replied, "Yes, you can, but only when your sisters and your mothers do what those Sisters are doing in there."

Later, when one of the many priests at the Kali Temple came down with tuberculosis, the Sisters took him in and cared for him with the same kindness and cordiality as all the other sick people. Every day, one of his brother priests came to visit him. Thus the Hindu priests at the nearby Kali Temple slowly became a circle of friends and supporters of Nirmal Hriday.

Mother Teresa had a deep respect for all human beings regarding their beliefs and their religions. She never tried to force or impose the Catholic Faith on anyone. Moreover, I think that what she left us was not so much a doctrine as its fruit: love in action—a heart full of love and hands that put that love into practice.

It was especially moving to observe how she touched the seriously ill and the dying, how she was not afraid to caress them—as a mother fondles her child's head and holds its hand. How often she changed human hearts and human lives through her touch! I do not know whether any of Mother Teresa's Hindu or Muslim coworkers ever changed their religion, but I am certain that there are thousands of human beings who changed their lives after an encounter with Mother Teresa.

Mother Teresa's great influence on the many people who met her became clear to me for the first time in the case of a high-ranking Indian police officer who accompanied us on a long trip. At first I did not like him at all; he appeared to be a know-it-all and gave instructions rudely. He made it plain to us that he wanted no part in religious matters and was only doing his duty. On the second day he already seemed considerably mellower. After Mother Teresa had given a short speech at one of our stops along the way, we took a short break before continuing our high-speed drive to the airport. At the end of the short break, the policemen asked if they could say goodbye to Mother Teresa there. The officer who had been so unlikeable at the start was no longer arrogant or aloof. Big tears rolled down his cheeks as he touched Mother Teresa's feet in the traditional Indian darshan (respectful farewell) and asked for her blessing. Mother Teresa offered them just one sentence from the Bible: "When they see your good works, may they give glory to God who is in heaven" (Mt 5:16).

In the car on the way to the airport, I had a lesson from Mother Teresa: "Father, our witness for Christ must always be of such a kind that people cannot decide against Him by mistake!" This was the kind of witness that Mother Teresa herself gave to countless people whom she met. The police officer dealt with all the formalities for us and even accompanied us till we boarded the plane, but now everything he did came from his heart, perhaps clumsily and overexuberantly, but with joy and gratitude.

ༀ

At the National Prayer Breakfast in the United States in 1994, Mother Teresa said,

I had the most extraordinary experience of love of neighbor from a Hindu family. A gentleman came to our house and said: "Mother Teresa, there is a family who have not eaten for so long. Do something." So I took some rice and went there immediately. And I saw the children, their eyes shining with hunger. I don't know if you have ever seen hunger, but I have seen it very often. And the mother of the family took the rice I gave her and went out. When she came back, I asked her: "Where did you go? What did you do?" And she gave me a very simple answer: "They are hungry also." What struck me was that she knew—and who were they? A Muslim family—and she knew. I didn't bring any more rice that evening because I wanted them, Hindus and Muslims, to enjoy the joy of sharing.[1]

As a Catholic priest, I was very interested in seeing how Mother Teresa understood Jesus' order to bring the Good News to the whole world, and how she herself lived it out. I think it can be summarized like this: There is only one God, and He is the God of all. That is why, in our humanity, we are all equal in God's sight. To Mother Teresa it was important that the example that she and her Sisters offered should help all people to come closer to God. It should cause Hindus to become better Hindus, Muslims to become better Muslims, and Catholics to become better Catholics. Mother Teresa did not so much emphasize the doctrines of the Catholic Church; rather, she stressed the importance of putting the greatest possible love into the actions we do.

It is said that a minister of the Mengistu Communist dictatorship in Ethiopia once asked Mother Teresa whether

---

[1] Mother Teresa, Address at the National Prayer Breakfast (Washington, D.C., February 3, 1994), www.catholic.org/clife/teresa/address.php.

she would try to preach there too and also whether she would try to convert people, which was strictly forbidden. Prudently, she did not address the question directly but just said, "Our works of charity show the poor and the suffering the love that God has for them."

Mother Teresa was truly a missionary, and at the same time she had a big heart for all people, regardless of their beliefs or their religious affiliations. This is not a contradiction but forms a consistent whole and shows the strength of her personality. For example, when she received an honorary doctorate in Madras, the rector, the dean, a professor from the university and finally the archbishop of Madras all appeared as speakers during the ceremony. They all spoke about the social involvement and commitment of their honored guest. I was very keen to hear what she herself would say, for not one of the previous speakers had even mentioned Jesus in his speech. For me the one interesting question was this: Would Mother Teresa, too, in this predominantly Muslim and Hindu setting, refrain from speaking about Jesus because it might cause problems?

For this ceremonial occasion they had draped a red cloak around her. She walked up onto the platform and climbed onto a little stool that they had placed for her behind the lectern, because she was so small. She still had to crane her neck in order to be able to see anything at all over the lectern. Then she pulled the microphone down to her level. Suddenly everyone was quiet as mice. During the earlier speeches, the fifteen thousand people in the audience had talked uninhibitedly. Only the loudspeakers had drowned out the loud noise they made. But the moment Mother Teresa took the microphone, there was total silence.

Into this silence she began, in her soft, deep voice, to say her first sentence: "Jesus loved the world so much that. . ." And then she gave a perfectly normal catechism lesson about love, in very simple terms, of course, mindful of the Hindus and Muslims who were present. She wanted to show them that their love for their neighbor, for the poorest of the poor, is love for God Himself.

As a missionary, she had nothing to proclaim but Jesus Himself. Always, especially when she herself was being honored, it was important to her to point away from herself. She wanted to draw people's attention, not to herself, but to God. When she finished her speech in Madras, there was complete silence in the auditorium. In this respectful, almost reverent atmosphere, everyone left. No one was talking any longer, and the silence was almost a palpable sign of the honor in which they held Mother Teresa.

In the middle of a predominantly Hindu environment, Mother Teresa was an outstanding missionary, in giving herself entirely to Jesus and in her willingness to encounter Him in the poorest of the poor of that country. For her, conversion meant bringing people closer to God through love. The love, tenderness and cheerfulness of the Missionaries of Charity create the occasion and the place where the Spirit of God and the soul of a person can meet. Thus, for Mother Teresa every act of love was always directed toward the conversion of a soul. "We are not social workers; we are contemplatives in the world," she used to say.

India is a federal republic, and in many of its states there are restrictive religious laws that forbid conversion to another religion. Asked whether she converted people, Mother Teresa once answered, "I hope that I convert people, but by that I do not mean what you are thinking. I hope that we convert hearts. Not even Almighty God can convert a human being if he does not want it. What we are trying to do by our work, by our service to people, is to come closer to God. Conversion must be understood in just this sense. Many think that converting means changing overnight, but it is not that. If we go into God's presence face-to-face and let Him into our life, then we are being converted."

Trusting in God's grace more than in her own abilities was certainly an essential trait of Mother Teresa. Once, among the passengers on a flight over Panama was the then archbishop of Panama, Marcos Gregorio McGrath, who was a very tall, imposing man. As we were flying over the jungle, a gigantic white dome suddenly towered above the dense foliage. The Archbishop explained to Mother Teresa that it was a central Bahá'i Temple. She responded spontaneously, "Father, do you have the medals?"

19

A Voice for the Voiceless

MOTHER TERESA not only preached against abortion; she also tried in very concrete ways to save unborn lives. "We fight abortion through adoption" was her axiom. That is why she wanted to take care of every child for whom she could get permission to do so, as for example in the Soviet Union, a country with extremely high abortion rates. There she was allowed to select twelve children from a list. Next to the name and age of each child was noted his or her handicap or, for the most seriously handicapped, just one word—"idiot"—that meant "incapable of life."

Mother Teresa said, "I will take all the children who are 'incapable of life.'" Among them were Sergei and Alexei. Sergei was a boy with a tiny emaciated body who did not walk but could only drag himself along the floor, suffering terribly all the while. Later it turned out that he simply had a tendon that was too short. He was completely neglected and half-starved because in the orphanage he did not manage to scoot quickly enough to the soup pot, so he regularly lost out when food was distributed. A surgeon performed an operation on Sergei's tendon and solved the problem.

Very early on, the Sisters brought the children who were in need of a massage to massage therapy. At first the masseuse did not want to touch the boys. Like many Russians, she was of the opinion that such children are of no use to society and therefore had no right to live.

Alexei, in the beginning, was considered rather a "naughty" child. The Sisters said that he was unhappy because he realized that his birth mother had mistreated him and given him away. Like all the children, he wore a Miraculous Medal on a string around his neck. The Sisters explained to him that from now on, the Mother of God would be his mother. From that moment on, Alexei was the best-behaved child at the midday meal; he would kiss his medal over and over again. When he was getting dressed, anyone who tried to help him had to kiss the medal first; only then could they touch him.

The masseuse changed too. She was curious when she saw the medal. The next day the Sisters gave her one for herself. From then on she was glad when the handicapped children came, and treated Alexei especially with great love, care and respect.

When I went briefly back to Moscow in the 1990's, a family from Novosibirsk had just been found that wanted to adopt Alexei. The adoption procedures were very complicated, and a doctor had to examine and question Alexei. Alexei answered his questions in both Russian and English, which he had learned from the Sisters. Finally, when Alexei asked the doctor why he was asking all those stupid questions, the latter looked thoughtfully for a long time at the certificate that said that Alexei was an "idiot" (in Russian, "incapable of living"), then tore it up and gave a green light for the adoption. In Novosibirsk Alexei became a zealous altar server for Bishop Werth. Today the boy who was "incapable of living" is studying at university.

We often encountered very seriously handicapped children. Among them were several terribly deformed infants with elephantiasis, completely swollen faces or missing limbs. Often I was horrified and would have preferred to turn away. Mother Teresa only said, "What a wonderful child!"

To her it was clear that a ray of God's light comes into the world even through severely handicapped children. Every child is a gift from God. The joy, the cheerfulness and the loving care that Mother Teresa showed children and very small babies made a great impression on us. I often thought that if God treats us as tenderly, as cheerfully and with as much joyful hope as Mother Teresa treats these little children, I still have a chance. To Mother Teresa, it was the most obvious thing in the world to accept every child with love.

That was probably the secret of her success: the power of tenderness. People were not touched by her because of any special intellectual accomplishments or her exemplary social achievements, but because they saw that she treated people with so much tenderness, empathy and self-sacrifice. What touches people's hearts is when they feel how much they are loved. For Mother Teresa this was simply passing on the love that God had given her.

She accepted people whom we usually find rather repulsive with the same esteem as she gave to us. She spoke no differently with the president of a nation than with a prostitute, no differently with a Carmelite nun than with Muhammad Ali, the world champion boxer who visited her in Calcutta. For many people this must have been a huge surprise—as it will probably be for us, too, when, one day in heaven, we experience God's goodness face-to-face, something we do not understand rationally.

Such goodness is deeply moving. When Mother Teresa welcomed groups of visitors and spoke with them for twenty minutes, often half of them went out afterward weeping or with tears in their eyes. Mother Teresa lived the powerlessness, indeed the helplessness, of love. She never tried to force anyone; she simply wanted to wrap other people in the web of love.

တ

For this reason she found it all the more terrible that many parents reject their own child, that many children are "unwanted." Again and again she warned, not only in personal conversations, but before the eyes and ears of the world, "Abortion is murder in the mother's womb. A child is a gift from God. If you do not want it, then give it to me. I want it."

Mother Teresa received the Nobel Peace Prize in 1979. She used the opportunity of her Nobel lecture, with the attention of a broad, international public focused on her, to speak out vehemently against abortion. "I feel the greatest destroyer of peace today is abortion, because it is a direct war, a direct killing, direct murder by the mother herself. . . . Many people are very, very concerned with the children of India, with the children of Africa where quite a number die, maybe of malnutrition, of hunger and so on, but millions are dying deliberately by the will of the mother. And this is what is the greatest destroyer of peace today. Because if a mother can kill her own child, what is left [but] for me to kill you and you to kill me. There is nothing [in] between."[1]

---

[1]   Mother Teresa, Nobel Lecture (Nobel Peace Prize Ceremony, New York, December 11, 1979), http://nobelprize.org/nobel_prizes/peace/laureates/1979/teresa-lecture.html.

Those were very harsh words. The next day a priest who had heard her speech on the radio is said to have remonstrated with her; her words had offended many women in Scandinavia. Mother Teresa's response was characteristic. She reportedly looked the young priest in the eyes and said, "Father, Jesus said, 'I am the Truth', and it is your duty and mine to speak the truth. Then it is up to the person who hears it whether to accept or reject it."

Looking back I can say that Mother Teresa spoke the truth, whether it was convenient or inconvenient—but always with great love.

In her speech at the United Nations in 1985, which I have already mentioned, Mother Teresa made a passionate appeal for the protection of unborn human life. I quote here from a transcript of her speech:

> Works of love begin at home and works of love are works of peace. We all want peace, and yet, and yet we are frightened of nuclears [nuclear weapons], we are frightened of this new disease [AIDS]. But we are not afraid to kill an innocent child, that little unborn child, who has been created for that same purpose: to love God and to love you and me.
>
> This is what is such a contradiction, and today I feel that abortion has become the greatest destroyer of peace. We are afraid of the nuclears [nuclear weapons], because it is touching [i.e., affects] us, but we are not afraid, the mother is not afraid to commit that terrible murder. Even when God Himself speaks of that, He says, "Even if [a] mother could forget her child, I will not forget you. I have carved you on the palm of my hand, you are precious to me, I love you." These are God's own words to you, to me, to that little unborn child. And this is why if we really want peace, if we

are sincere in our hearts that we really want peace, today, let us make that strong resolution that in our countries, in our cities, we will not allow a single child to feel unwanted, to feel unloved, to [be] a throwaway [of] society. And let us help each other to strengthen that. That in our countries that terrible law of killing the innocents, of destroying life, destroying the presence of God, be removed from our country, from our nation, from our people, from our families.[2]

On February 3, 1994, in Washington, D.C., at the National Prayer Breakfast hosted by both Houses of Congress, the Senate and the House of Representatives, Mother Teresa stated her position in equally clear language. Here are extensive excerpts from her speech:

God loved the world so much that He gave His Son—it was a giving. God gave His Son to the Virgin Mary, and what did she do with Him? As soon as Jesus came into Mary's life, immediately she went in haste to give that good news. And as she came into the house of her cousin, Elizabeth, Scripture tells us that the unborn child—the child in the womb of Elizabeth—leapt with joy. While still in the womb of Mary, Jesus brought peace to John the Baptist who leapt for joy in the womb of Elizabeth. The unborn was the first one to proclaim the coming of Christ.

And as if that were not enough, as if it were not enough that God the Son should become one of us and bring peace and joy while still in the womb of Mary, Jesus also died on the Cross to show that greater love. He died for you and for me, and for that leper and for that man dying of hunger and

---

[2]   Mother Teresa, "One Strong Resolution: I Will Love" (Address to the United Nations, New York, October 26, 1985).

that naked person lying in the street, not only of Calcutta, but of Africa, and everywhere. Our Sisters serve these poor people in 105 countries throughout the world. Jesus insisted that we love one another as He loves each one of us. Jesus gave His life to love us. . . . Jesus says very clearly: "Love as I have loved you." . . .

Maybe in our own family we have somebody who is feeling lonely, who is feeling sick, who is feeling worried. Are we there? Are we there to be with them, or do we merely put them in the care of others? Are we willing to give until it hurts in order to be with our families, or do we put our own interests first? . . .

I was surprised in the West to see so many young boys and girls given to drugs. And I tried to find out why. Why is it like that, when those in the West have so many more things than those in the East? And the answer was: "Because there is no one in the family to receive them." Our children depend on us for everything—their health, their nutrition, their security, their coming to know and love God. For all of this, they look to us with trust, hope and expectation. But often father and mother are so busy they have no time for their children, or perhaps they are not even married or have given up on their marriage. So their children go to the streets and get involved in drugs or other things. We are talking of love of the child, which is w[h]ere love and peace must begin. These are the things that break peace.

But I feel that the greatest destroyer of peace today is abortion, because it is a war against the child, a direct killing of the innocent child, murder by the mother herself. And if we accept that a mother can kill even her own child, how can we tell other people not to kill one another? How do we persuade a woman not to have an abortion? As always, we must persuade her with love and we remind ourselves that love means to be willing to give until it hurts. Jesus gave even His life to love us. So, the mother who is thinking of abortion, should be helped to love, that is, to give until it hurts her plans, or her free time, to respect the life of her child. The father of that child, whoever he is, must also give until it hurts.

By abortion, the mother does not learn to love, but kills even her own child to solve her problems. And, by abortion, that father is told that he does not have to take any responsibility at all for the child he has brought into the world. The father is likely to put other women into the same trouble. So abortion just leads to more abortion. Any country that accepts abortion is not teaching its people to love, but to use any violence to get what they want. This is why the greatest destroyer of love and peace is abortion.

Many people are very, very concerned with the children of India, with the children of Africa where quite a few die of hunger, and so on. Many people are also concerned about all the violence in this great country of the United States. These concerns are very good. But often these same people are not concerned with the millions who are being killed by the deliberate decision of their own mothers. And this is what is the greatest destroyer of peace today—abortion which brings people to such blindness.[3]

Mother Teresa did not say any of this to judge the women, who are often under enormous pressure from the people around them. First of all she wanted to recall the dignity of

[3]   Mother Teresa, (Address at National Prayer Breakfast, Washington DC, February 3, 1994).

the child. Every child is a gift, created in God's image, "to love and to be loved." And then she would point out her own way of fighting against abortion: "I will tell you something beautiful. We are fighting abortion by adoption."

On another occasion, Mother Teresa told American political and business leaders about a small child whom she had arranged for a married couple to adopt. When it turned out that the child was seriously ill, she told the adoptive parents, "Give me the sick child back. I will give you a healthy one instead."

But the adoptive father replied, "Mother Teresa you will have to take my life first, only then can you take the child from me."

This sick child brought so much love and joy to that family. She added, "And so I make this offer to you, too, in the presence of our Sisters: Whoever does not want their child, please give it to me. I want it."

The Missionaries of Charity have saved the lives of thousands of children in this way through their adoption services. I quote further from Mother Teresa's speech at the National Prayer Breakfast: "I am willing to accept any child who would be aborted and to give that child to a married couple who will love the child and be loved by the child. From our children's home in Calcutta alone, we have saved over 3,000 children from abortion. These children have brought such love and joy to their adopting parents and have grown up so full of love and joy."

Mother Teresa also made it clear that while she would accept every child, she did not accept all couples as adoptive parents. "I know that couples have to plan their family and for that there is natural family planning. The way to plan the family is natural family planning, not contraception." She explained that in artificial contraception the attention of the husband is concentrated entirely on himself and the wife's on herself. In love, however, the attention of the husband and the wife must be directed toward each other, and this is what happens in natural family planning. Mother Teresa also said, "We cannot solve all the problems in the world, but let us never bring in the worst problem of all, and that is to destroy love. And this is what happens when we tell people to practice contraception and abortion."

In this historic speech at the National Prayer Breakfast, which is one of the very few talks that she prepared carefully in writing beforehand, Mother Teresa placed the phenomenon of abortion within the wider context of the spiritual poverty of our societies. "Abortion, which often follows from contraception, brings a people to be spiritually poor, and that is the worst poverty and the most difficult to overcome." At the end of her speech she called on her listeners to do everything possible "that no child will be unwanted, unloved, uncared for, or killed and thrown away."

ᴄᴏ

Less well publicized, but no less genuine, was Mother Teresa's loving concern for those women who suffered under the burden of a past abortion. Such women belonged to a little circle of privileged persons whom Mother Teresa embraced with heartfelt love and in a special way. I saw many young women with tear-stained faces who, after a meeting with Mother Teresa, were once again each able to trust in the love and forgiveness of God that Mother Teresa had just shown her so tangibly; it is that kind of love that restores people's hope of reconciliation and of being able to lead a happy life again.

For Mother Teresa, the sanctity of the lives of children, these "rays of God's light in the world," was absolutely inviolable and must be defended in every situation. But she also understood people's material and social needs, the abandonment and loneliness they feel in those difficult moments when they make their decision. She always had an open mind, open arms and a wide-open heart for the victims of this spiritual dilemma.

20

It Is His Work!

WHAT MADE MOTHER TERESA so totally immune to all the temptations that she must have faced to become proud, conceited or vain because of the recognition and honors, awards and distinctions, meetings with great statesmen and endless small privileges that she experienced? Why, despite all the fuss that was made over her, did she always remain the unassuming "pencil in God's hand," His humble servant?

"It is His work!" she once said, with her index finger pointing upward, to a journalist who commented that her accomplishments throughout the world were beyond marvelous. She reacted similarly to questions about whether all the praise and awards that she received—she had probably received more honors than anyone else on the planet—did not make her even a little bit proud. She would point one index finger to each ear and say, "It goes in here and out the other side again. And there is nothing in between. It is His work!"

When Mother Teresa received yet another honorary doctorate from an Indian university, she said to a bishop who was traveling with her, "I have never studied or received a diploma. I don't know much about human laws; I know only a little about divine laws, and, whoosh, already I am getting so many honorary doctorates."

On October 26, 1985, Mother Teresa was invited to speak to the General Assembly of the United Nations in New York. On the day of the speech, she followed the normal routine at her Sisters' house in Washington. After Holy Mass and the morning hour of Adoration came the regular cleaning: first, washing her sari, then cleaning the toilets and the floors. As on any other day she set an example by working alongside the other Sisters. She usually focused on cleaning the toilets: "I am a specialist in that, probably the world's best specialist in cleaning toilets."

Then she was driven to New York in the elderly car of a volunteer who worked with her congregation. When she entered the main building of the United Nations, she was greeted by the delegates and heads of state with a standing ovation.

U.N. General Secretary Javier Pérez de Cuéllar introduced her as follows:

> This is a hall of words. A few days ago we had, in this rostrum, the most powerful men in the world. Now we have the privilege to have the most powerful woman in the world. I don't think I need to present her. She doesn't need words. She does need deeds. I think that the best thing I can do is to pay tribute to her and to tell [say] that she is much more than I, much more than all of us. She is the United Nations. She is peace in this world. Thank you.[1]

[1] Javier Peréz de Cuéllar, Introduction of Mother Teresa (United Nations, New York, October 26, 1985), http://www.piercedhearts.org/purity_heart_morality/mother_teresa_address_united_nations.htm.

Mother Teresa walked through the General Assembly hall to the speaker's podium and began her speech:

> We have gathered together to thank God for the 40 years of the beautiful work that the United Nations have put in for the good of the people, and as we begin the Year of Peace, let us say the prayer, you have all got one, we say the prayer together for peace. For works of love are works of peace. We say it together so that we may obtain peace and God can give us peace, by uniting us together.[2]

And there she was, leading a prayer in the middle of that hall of world politics and global political intrigue:

> Make us worthy, Lord, to serve our fellow men throughout
>   the world, who live and die in poverty and hunger.
> Give them through our hands, this day, their daily bread
>   and by our understanding love give peace and joy.
>
> Lord, make me a channel of thy peace.
> That where there is hatred I may bring love,
> That where there is wrong, I may bring the spirit of
>   forgiveness,
> That where there is discord, I may bring harmony,
> That where there is error I may bring truth,
> That where there is doubt I may bring faith,
> That where there is despair I may bring hope,
> That where there are shadows I may bring light,
> That where there is sadness I may bring joy.
> Lord, grant that I may seek rather to comfort than to be
>   comforted,

---

[2]   Mother Teresa, "One Strong Resolution: I Will Love" (Address to the United Nations, October 26, 1985).

To understand than to be understood,
To love than to be loved.
For it is by forgetting self that one finds.
It is by forgiving that one is forgiven,
It is by dying that one awakens to eternal life.
Amen.[3]

She began her speech with this prayer by Saint Francis of Assisi. And then she gave the politicians and diplomats who were gathered there a perfectly normal catechism lesson, in which she—as always—pointed away from herself and toward Jesus:

> We have asked our Lord to make us channels of peace, of joy, of love, of unity, and this is why Jesus came: to prove that love. God loved the world so much that He gave Jesus His Son to come among us, to give us that good news, that God loves us. And that He wants us to love one another as He loves each one of us. That He has created us for that one reason: to love and to be loved. No other reason. We are not just a number in the world. We are children of God.[4]

In her speech, she said that when she was in China she had been asked, "What is a Communist to you?" And she answered, "My brother, my sister." Then turning again to the delegates, she said,

> And exactly that is what you and I are meant to be: brother, sister. Because the same loving hand of God [that] has created you, created me, created [the] man of the street, created that leper, that hungry man, that rich man, for that

---

[3] Ibid.
[4] Ibid.

same purpose: to love and to be loved. And this is what you and I have come together today to find: the means of peace.[5]

I mentioned earlier that in this highly regarded speech she described abortion as "the greatest destroyer of peace," and how she recalled the needs of the family. But we should also not overlook the appeal she made to the heads of state, ambassadors and delegates who were present:

And so today, when we have gathered here together, let us carry in our hearts one strong resolution: I will love. I will be a carrier of God's love. . . .

Let us love again, so let us share, let us pray that this terrible suffering be removed from our people. . . . I will pray for you that you may grow in this love of God, by loving one another as He loves each one of you, and especially that through this love, you become holy. Holiness is not a luxury of the few. It's a simple duty for each one of us. For holiness brings love, and love brings peace, and peace brings us together.

And let us not be afraid, for God is with us if we allow Him, if we give Him the joy of a pure heart.[6]

She concluded her speech before the U.N. General Assembly with the following thought:

Prayer will give us a clean heart, and a clean heart will allow us to see God in each other. And if we see God in each other, we will be able to live in peace, and if we live in peace, we will be able to share the joy of loving with each other, and God will be with us.[7]

---

[5] Ibid.
[6] Ibid.
[7] Ibid.

When her appearance at the United Nations was over—she had dispensed with a banquet so that the money might go to the poor—the elderly model car in which she had come to New York drove her back to the Sisters' house in Washington, where she continued to follow the routine and schedule of the house, just like all the Sisters.

It is possible that Mother Teresa also had to fight to keep this modesty and simplicity against her own temptations.

Her toilet cleaning, which I have already mentioned, also had spiritual significance, as the following story that I heard illustrates. On an overseas flight to Washington to visit the then U.S. president Ronald Reagan, one of the Sisters who was accompanying her noticed something odd: Mother Teresa went into the toilet at the front of the business-class section, first into the one on the right, then into the one on the left. Then she walked to the back of the plane to the other toilets. The Sister's curiosity won out over her embarrassment and she asked Mother Teresa the reason for these repeated trips to the toilets. Her brief answer was, "Exorcism!"

Mother Teresa had cleaned all the toilets, and it seems that it was precisely in cleaning the toilets that she found an antidote to any hint of pride. This would fit well with the maxim that she often repeated: "How do you learn humility? Only through humiliations!"

❧

In the chapel at the Motherhouse in Calcutta—in addition to the crucifix with the words "I thirst" under Jesus' right arm, the altar and a lectern—there was a large statue of the Mother of God. This was decorated with a Distinguished Service Medal that Mother Teresa had received from the queen of England. She also used to hang other medals around the statue from time to time. This is a good image for the way in which Mother Teresa accepted all the many honors, medals and distinctions that were awarded to her, as a representative of the poorest of the poor and, at the same time, in the knowledge that not one of those honors was something that she herself had earned. She never grew tired of emphasizing that everything was "His work." And because she was totally oriented toward Jesus, she constantly acted and lived in an intimate relationship with Mary, His Mother. Incidentally, she sent the queen of England a photo of the Madonna wearing the British medal, to show her that it was being put to good use.

At the feet of the Mother of God, who stood on a pedestal, there was a free space. There Mother Teresa placed a silver dove of peace—another award that she had received. Of course, when an award included an endowment she gladly accepted the money—for the poorest of the poor. If medals had some material value, for instance if they were made of gold, she would usually sell them so as to give the money to the poor.

The list of awards she received for her work is very long; the following are just a few. The president of India awarded her the Padma Shri in 1962. The same year she received the Ramon Magsaysay Award from the president of the Philippines. In 1971 she received the Pope John XXIII Peace Prize from the hands of Pope Paul VI in Rome, and the John F. Kennedy International Award in New York. One year later she received the Good Samaritan Award in Boston and an honorary doctorate from the Catholic University of America in Washington. That year the Indian government also granted her the Jawaharlal Nehru Award for International

Understanding. On April 25, 1973, Prince Philip presented her with the Templeton Prize for Progress in Religion in London. On October 17, 1979, she accepted the Nobel Peace Prize in Oslo. The following year, she was given India's highest civilian award, the Bharat Ratna. In 1985 she was honored with the Presidential Medal of Freedom, the highest honor granted to a civilian by the United States. In 1991 she was able to travel to Albania for the first time, and to participate in the reconsecration of the Catholic cathedral there. In 1992 she was granted honorary Albanian citizenship. In 1996 she became an honorary citizen of the United States.

In the extremely frugally furnished room in which Mother Teresa lived when she was in Calcutta there were, in addition to a bed and a writing desk, a large number of cardboard boxes standing on a bookcase that were labeled Outgoing Mail, Incoming Mail, Sister Y, and, finally, Awards. At the end of each trip, Mother Teresa would put the awards that she had received into the Awards box. When it was full, the awards were emptied into a larger metal box. Today, in the archives of the Motherhouse in Calcutta, next to the room where Mother Teresa is buried, there are seven simple army lockers full of the awards and medals with which she was honored, and a collection of the stamps that bear her likeness from almost every country in the world.

It was fascinating to see how Mother Teresa was little concerned about her own image. She knew that "at the end of our life we will not be judged on how many diplomas we received or how much money we made or how many great things we accomplished. At the end of our life this is how we will be judged: 'I was hungry and you gave me food, I was naked and you clothed me, I was homeless and you welcomed me'" (Mt 25:35–36).

Failures or partial successes were therefore not crises for her but gave her a deep, inner peace. "You see, Father," she usually began her little lectures, "God didn't call me to be successful. God called me to be faithful." Thus failures and disappointments were also Mother Teresa's constant companions.

Apparently she once said, "I know that God will not impose on me anything that I cannot bear. But sometimes I wish that He did not have such great confidence in me."

☙

In 1988 I was given a computer for Christmas. That was not such a routine thing then as it is today. Besides, it was the most up-to-date model and had two drives! When the planning began for the opening of a house in Russia, I thought my computer would be very useful so I wanted to take it with me to Moscow. Mother Teresa listened carefully to my plan and my arguments. Then she looked at me firmly and said, "Father, it is better not to take it along. It is better simply to perform humble service." I was dumbfounded. And in that silence she said, "Father, do you know how one learns humility? Only through humiliations."

Looking back, this sacrifice had two positive results. Firstly, all my luggage went missing on the way to Moscow, so I would have lost the computer; secondly, I discovered that Mother Teresa, although it was important to her to teach her principles, could still be very flexible when confronted with practical situations. Many months later, during Easter 1989 (I had almost completely forgotten about the computer), Mother Teresa called me in Armenia and said, "Father, if you want, you can now have them send your computer." Although months had passed, she remembered how much willpower it had cost me not to bring it along. Perhaps, though, she also thought that by then I had learned what I was meant to learn.

At the end of my time in Armenia I sold the computer to a wealthy Armenian for all of $13,500; the artificial exchange rate of roubles to dollars at the time was one to one. With the proceeds we were able to finance a trip to Paris and Rome for a whole group of Armenian young people.

My brother also once gave me one of the first mobile phones as a gift. Back then this consisted of a bag that contained a receiver. The whole thing weighed about six pounds. But it was portable, at least, and of course I could use it to organize things for the Sisters and for Mother Teresa herself. Perhaps I also wanted, just a little, to impress Mother Teresa with it.

The only technological appliance that Mother Teresa and her Sisters used in their houses was the telephone. Mobile phones must also be permitted in that category, I thought. So I suggested to Mother Teresa that she should equip at least the superiors of each house, or of each region, with a mobile phone. In view of the Sisters' vow of poverty, I thought my argument was rather clever: "You know, you could save a lot of money with it, because you could be reached everywhere and you could avoid a lot of unnecessary journeys by making a simple, short call from one of these mobile phones." Lower costs!

Mother Teresa simply said, "Father, we have a vow of poverty, not a vow of economy."

21

Suffering and Death

IN A DOCUMENTARY FILM by the sisters Jeanette and Ann Petrie, Mother Teresa is asked how it is possible to understand suffering. She says, "Suffering by itself has no meaning. . . . But suffering shared with the suffering of Christ has a tremendous meaning. The suffering offered as a reparation has a tremendous meaning. . . . Suffering is really the most beautiful way of growing in holiness to be like Jesus."

This acceptance and offering-up do not only apply to major suffering or almost unbearable loss. Making small sacrifices for God out of minor things that happen at school, at work or in our family can shape our whole lives. An example demonstrates how Mother Teresa thoroughly disliked being the center of interest. She was even less fond of being photographed. However, because she could hardly avoid it, she made a "contract with heaven," as she used to say; for every photo taken of her, she asked Jesus to release a soul from purgatory and bring it to heaven. Thus she managed to offer up the tiresome business of being photographed. When she arrived at an airport, a platform was often built, either beside the runway or in the reception area, for the photographers who were waiting for her. As soon as she got there a veritable storm of flashing cameras would begin. When this went on for a very long time, she would say with a broad smile, "That's enough; purgatory is empty."

Once, she jokingly explained that the current rate of inflation was so high that she, too, had changed her "contract": "Now two souls will have to go to heaven from purgatory for every photo that is taken of me."

Many people who knew Mother Teresa or her Sisters were impressed by their cheerfulness; it was infectious, despite the difficult circumstances in which the Sisters themselves usually lived and worked. In the rules for her communities, Mother Teresa defined the kind of spirit they should have. She emphasized three points: first, "loving trust," then, "total surrender," and finally, "cheerfulness!" For her, these three points were closely interconnected: If I have loving trust in God, if I can surrender myself to Him completely, then cheerfulness is almost a logical consequence. For Mother Teresa, loving trust meant trust in God's plan, to which she surrendered herself entirely in all her "nothingness," her insignificance—"nothingness" was a key word that she often used. God could change this nothingness into something, but that was "His work," and not the result of our own efforts.

Conversely, she once said that even God cannot fill something that is already full. By this she meant that if we are full of self, of vanity and our own selfish goals, if we think that we can do everything by ourselves, God cannot work with us; He cannot use us. But when we accept our "nothingness" and turn to Him with loving trust, then He can use us; He can fill us with His love and do "great things" with us.

Closely connected with this is "total surrender," submission to God's will. Mother Teresa also used the word "belonging" to describe this. If I surrender myself totally to Jesus, I belong to Him. She told her Sisters who had not yet taken their vows, "When you take your vows, then you belong totally to Jesus and must hold fast to Jesus; you must cling to Him. Allow no one to come between you and Jesus."

A priest once told me the following story, which shows how seriously she took this closeness to Jesus. When Mother Teresa was in the hospital, suffering a great deal and in severe pain, one of the doctors asked her, "Mother Teresa, what I do not understand is why you have to suffer so much."

She replied, "Because He (Jesus) Himself suffered so much and because I belong to Him. If I must die tomorrow, good. He can use me as He wants. I have no choice of my own."

With this total surrender Mother Teresa lived out another sentence from her community's statutes: Total surrender consists, among other things, in "accepting whatever He gives and giving whatever He takes away, with a big smile." Belonging to Jesus means, for Mother Teresa and her Sisters, that He can use them however and for whatever purpose He pleases, "without being consulted"—without asking their permission first.

One consequence of this loving trust and total surrender is cheerfulness. When cheerfulness is fed from these sources it is a fruit of the Holy Spirit and an essential mark of the Kingdom of God. Cheerfulness is a net with which we can catch souls. A Sister who overflows with cheerfulness teaches without speaking. "A cheerful Sister," Mother Teresa used to say, "is like a sunbeam of God's love. She is a ray of hope in eternal happiness. She is a flame of burning love."

༉

One evening, after a very hot and strenuous day in Central India, Bishop Hnilica and I were sitting down and having a long and much-needed drink of water to replenish the fluids we had lost during the day. Mother Teresa and her Sisters were praying in another room. Mother Teresa came in when they had finished, and one of us said, to justify himself a little for resting and drinking instead of praying, "Today really was a miracle! How can so much be packed into one day?!" Disregarding the mild rebuke, she answered with a beaming smile, "Father, the miracle is not the work that we do. The miracle is that we are happy to be able to do it."

This miracle of doing one's duty happily, despite the misery and suffering all around, springs from seeing the world from a spiritual point of view. When I saw Mother Teresa for the first time after I was ordained, in the chapel of the Missionaries of Charity in the Villa San Gregorio in Rome, the first thing she said to me was: "Father, when you celebrate your Mass, please put a drop of water for me into the chalice."

By that I believe she meant: When you pour the drop of water into the chalice, take me into the Mystery of the Consecration.

From then on I did something else: While placing a fragment of the Host into the chalice—symbolizing the Resurrection—I always included Mother Teresa. But, looking back, the meaning of her request becomes even clearer to me. Now that we know about her "dark night of the soul," the painful trial in which she was deprived of any sense of God's presence, I understand her request thus: that I should put the drop of water, which symbolizes mankind, into Christ's divinity—in other words, into the wine that is transformed into Christ's Blood, so that through it she would be taken up completely into God. I think that is what she wanted to ask me—to remind God again and again that she was totally enveloped and absorbed in Him. This also corresponds precisely with the prayer that the priest says during Mass at the mingling of the water and wine.

Even at a young age, Mother Teresa understood that her particular way of imitating Christ was bound up with her own suffering. For many long years she shared the burden of Jesus' sense of being utterly abandoned in the Garden of Gethsemane. Anyone who reads the book edited by Father Brian Kolodiejchuk, *Mother Teresa: Come, Be My Light*, will discover the distress of her abandonment.

Toward the end of her final illness, too, Mother Teresa had to undergo suffering that she herself must surely have directly associated with this painful sense of being abandoned by God. Because she was short of breath and her heart was not working properly—it often functioned at less than 50 percent of the norm—the circulation of blood to her brain was reduced and she had hallucinations.

One morning she asked the Sisters looking after her why all her Sisters had gone away the previous night. "Why did all the Sisters leave me? I was alone the whole night, and I so urgently needed the Sisters. No one was there." The Sisters had of course been there, but she thought they had all left her. She thought her congregation had turned against her. Her delusion can be completely explained in physical terms—but what tremendous suffering she must have endured.

Not only in the Home for the Dying, but also on many other occasions, Mother Teresa was directly confronted with the tragedy of death. She always spoke about death as "going back home to God." She had no fear at all of death and also no anxiety or hesitancy about the deaths of other people. A Sister from the AIDS residence in New York once told me that Mother Teresa said to Ben, an AIDS patient who was already near death, "Ben, I want you to wait for me at the gate of heaven and greet me when I arrive." She wanted to take away his fear of death, and Ben promised to do as she asked.

☙

For Mother Teresa there was nothing frightening about death because it was not far distant from life. I realized this when she sent me to Ethiopia to give a retreat for the Sisters. Before I left, I explained to Mother Teresa about the difficult political situation between Eritrea and Ethiopia, separated at that time by a demarcation line: "Some of the Sisters will have to cross the demarcation line between the enemy groups to come to the retreat, and that involves some risk. Do you have a special message for the Sisters who are putting their lives in danger there?"

Her answer may initially seem macabre, but it shows her light-hearted attitude toward death: "Yes, Father, tell them: If they must die, then they should die nicely."

I recall another story that Mother Teresa herself told. Shortly after she opened the first house of the Missionaries of Charity in Amman, the capital of the Kingdom of Jordan, in 1968, war broke out and there was fighting. The Sisters called Mother Teresa in Rome to tell her about the difficulties they were having. She encouraged them to trust in God and remain faithful to the poor. At the end of the conversation she said, "And call me again when you are dead."

In contrast, she was very distressed and shocked by a horrible accident that happened when she was in a private plane taking off from Dodoma in Tanzania. The small four-seater aircraft went into a tailspin immediately after lift-off and plunged into the crowd that had come to see her depart. One Missionary of Charity Sister and two other people were killed.

As though by a miracle, Mother Teresa herself was unharmed. As she got out of the plane, deeply upset, she murmured to herself, "God's will. God's will!" For several months she mourned, not only for her Sister, but also because other people who had come to honor her had lost their lives.

22

In the Prime of Her Holiness

I WAS SOMETIMES INTRODUCED as Mother Teresa's "confessor." That is not entirely correct. Wherever she was and whatever she was doing, Mother Teresa wanted a priest at her side because she did not want to miss daily Mass for herself and her Sisters or the opportunity for confession. I was merely privileged to be the "priest at her side" on several of her journeys and in several places. My only advantage was probably my availability. She also had other priests from other countries and continents, who had other histories and other talents.

I believe that, for her, every priest was also a person to be educated. She was able to teach him a lot as they worked together. A young priest—as I was at the beginning of our travels together—could still be trained, formed and corrected. After all, she had served with the Loreto Sisters as an instructor and a teacher and remained a gifted teacher all her life. Everything she did was a lesson.

I noticed one small example of this on many occasions. On car journeys, Mother Teresa would specify, as inconspicuously as possible, who should sit where. Thus, the Sisters were not allowed to sit beside a man, even if he was a priest. If the back seat held four people, a man could not sit there, only Sisters.

If there were three places on the back seat, a Sister would sit on the right, Mother Teresa in the middle, and the man on the left—that was quite clear. Since many, many of her Sisters were young, pretty, cheerful, charming Indian girls, this can certainly be seen as the prudent avoidance of temptation.

The funny thing was that, on such occasions, she herself would be the buffer: She would seat herself wherever she could prevent any temptation—even if only in her imagination—from arising. "Nobody and nothing," as she herself used to say, "should come between you and Jesus," and she would sit herself in the middle to make sure.

I think Mother Teresa was an expert in human nature and knew precisely what was going on around her. On the one hand, she had a natural wisdom that was not far removed from a farmer's shrewdness; on the other, however, she also had truly supernatural, mystical insights. And she was a virtuoso on the keyboard of human nature. There is no other explanation for the way she managed to think through and sort out so many problems and relationships in record time.

When there was discontent among her coworkers or those traveling with her, Mother Teresa would usually dissolve it promptly and intelligently with just a word or two. Once, after a really full day with hundreds of conversations and things to organize, I burst out, "Mother Teresa, traveling with a saint is really not at all easy."

She smiled and said, "You know, Father, who is a saint? A saint is someone who lives with a saint."

In human terms she was gifted, prudent and diplomatic, though perhaps she had not always been the latter. In the area of diplomacy she did learn a few things and matured with experience. In her first television interviews she still seems shy, inhibited and a bit defensive. Of course she always knew what she wanted to say, but now and then in the early years she sounded as though she was reciting it. She learned a lot and gained self-confidence. I was not there to witness these changes and so cannot describe them. I myself only knew her as a mature, fully developed personality—in the prime of her holiness. In all the years in which I was privileged to know her, I only noticed one change in her: She became increasingly mellow and loveable.

જી

The rare opportunities to see Mother Teresa after the evening meal and to speak with her in peace and quiet were partly taken up by practical and organizational questions. But once these were sorted out, everyone just wanted to listen to her. The conversation always developed along spiritual lines. She would seize the opportunity to tell us something instructive, edifying or amusing that, at the same time, always contained or described the miracle that God was for her.

In one such conversation the question arose: "What will it be like in heaven, and what will we be judged on?" She said, "I am not sure what heaven will be like. I believe that when we die and the time comes for us to be judged, God will not ask us how many good things we did in our life, but only with how much love we did them."

She surprised many people who critically questioned the credibility of the Church and thought they might find in her an ally for a revolution within it. She dealt with such schemers as she did with an apparently concerned journalist who asked, "Mother Teresa, what is wrong with the Church today?"

Like a pistol shot she retorted, "You and me!"

In her view, the real place where reform was constantly needed was in the heart of each individual.

Once a journalist tried to provoke her: "Mother Teresa, you're seventy now. When you die, the world will look exactly as it did before you were born. After all the effort you have made, what has changed in the world?"

Without a trace of impatience and with a winning smile she replied, "You know, I never wanted to change the world. I have only tried to be a drop of pure water in which God's love can be reflected. Does that seem a small thing to you?"

As often happened, the room fell silent. No one dared say anything. Mother Teresa turned to the reporter again and said, "Why don't you try, too, to be a drop of pure water? Then there would be two of us already. Are you married?"

"Yes, Mother Teresa."

"Tell your wife about it, too, and then we are already three. Do you have children?"

"Yes, three children, Mother Teresa."

"Then tell your children also, and then we are already six."

Nevertheless it's a good question: Is the effort that the Missionaries of Charity put in day after day worthwhile, if it is not possible to do away with misery? Mother Teresa once gave an excellent answer to this question to Archbishop Angelo Comastri. (He later became Vicar General of the Pope for the Vatican City and was elevated by Pope Benedict XVI to the rank of cardinal in 2007.) She said, "Yes, it is true. What we do is only a drop in the ocean. But without our work the ocean would be poorer by that drop."

I sometimes marveled at the people who had often waited for hours just to see Mother Teresa for a moment—or to touch her feet, as is the custom in India, or even to be able to speak a few words with her. They always left filled with joy and deeply moved. People from all classes and social groups in India longed to see her.

Archbishop Comastri once told a story that perhaps reveals something of what lay behind this longing. Once, on a flight with Mother Teresa, a man came up to him, got down on one knee beside him and said in a trembling voice, "Father, I don't understand what's happening. I feel as though God Himself were looking at me through the eyes of that woman."

Archbishop Comastri immediately went to Mother Teresa to tell her what the man had said. She replied with disarming calm, "Tell that man God has been looking at him for a long time. He just did not notice it. God is love."

Mother Teresa's "dark night of the soul," her unquenched thirst for the presence of God, has become known to a wide public through the documents published by Father Brian Kolodiejchuk. Precisely because of this, it seems to me important to emphasize that joy had a very special place in her life and work—not only the natural joy of a cheerful heart, but also intentional joy, the joy that one decides to feel.

The saying "If you don't smile, make a smile" shows that, for Mother Teresa, joy was not simply a reflection of our current mood; our mood is also influenced by our own will.

One day I brought Mother Teresa quite a large sum of money that I had been given and that I wanted to give her for the poor. She looked at the money in the envelope. Her first question was, "Father, are you happy giving me this money?"

To a group of her Sisters who were waiting at an airport, Mother Teresa once said, "If you meet someone who has no smile on his lips, give him one of your smiles."

Meditating out loud during a journey we made together, she said, "If we examine ourselves, we will notice that all temptations against purity, against the vow of chastity, happen when we are sad and moody. A moody Sister is a plaything in the hand of the devil. He can do with her whatever he wants. For if you are sad and moody, you will look around to see where you can satisfy your hunger for love. In order to stay chaste, you need the virtue of joy. Jesus willed 'that My joy may be yours.'"

Mother Teresa used to tell a story about a man who came into the House for the Dying in Calcutta without saying a word: "He just walked through the rows and then, when he went out again, he said to a Sister: 'I did not believe in God, but now I believe that there is a God, for only a God can give the Sisters so much love and joy in such terrible surroundings.'"

There is a similar story about three Muslims whom Mother Teresa brought into the House for the Dying. As she walked through the rows of the dying with them, she noticed that one of them had stayed behind. She left the other two, went back and saw that his eyes were full of tears. So she asked whether she could help him in any way. He said, "Mother Teresa, I have believed for my whole life that Jesus was a prophet, but today I know that He is God, because only God can give so much joy in caring for one's neighbor."

છ

After an acute phase in Mother Teresa's illness, all her Sisters and friends were very relieved that she was able to remain among us for a little while longer. Many of us spoke to her, either in veiled terms or openly, about the possibility that she was not yet ready for heaven.

"No, no, there's a different reason," she said. "I once dreamed that I had already arrived at the gate of heaven, but Saint Peter told me: Go back to earth; we have no slums up here."

She had replied: "Good, then I will go back to earth and fill heaven with poor people instead."

On another occasion, after surviving a serious and life-threatening illness, Mother Teresa came from Calcutta to Rome. Again and again she told anyone who would listen, "I had almost gone back home to God, but the prayers of the whole world, of my Sisters and of all the dear people—they kept me back. So many letters and cards with 'Get well soon' arrived each day at our house in Calcutta from all parts of the world—from thousands of people whom I do not know at all. You should see what beautiful drawings little children made for me, and the love in the letters that they write. I think that Saint Peter has grown tired of running back and forth to bring Jesus and Mary all the prayers that have been offered to them for me."

Saint Peter had clearly found it easier to let Mother Teresa recover.

Mother Teresa had several heart operations. But neither a weak heart nor well-meaning advice from her doctor could slow her down or keep her from taking on the burden of the routine of a full day's work.

Even in the hospital, a few months before her death, she did not lose her cheerfulness and sense of humor. Apparently, after she had been admitted one evening, she was hooked up to an ECG machine and connected to a whole bundle of cables. When she noticed them, she began to count them and asked a Sister, "What are all these cables doing here? Is it already Christmas that I should look like a Christmas tree?"

The Sister answered, "That's an ECG, Mother Teresa. A very lovely ornament, a pretty decoration." Mother Teresa looked at her hands, completely blue from the needles that had been stuck into them, and commented, "This, too, is a gift from God."

In March 1997 she was finally able to relinquish responsibility as general superior of her congregation. On August 30 that year, Lady Diana, whom Mother Teresa had met in 1985, died. She was invited to the funeral but could no longer travel because of her medical condition.

When Mother Teresa died on the evening of September 5, 1997, in Calcutta, her religious family, which consisted of five congregations, had 592 houses, or, more precisely, "tabernacles." Today there are more than 750 "tabernacles" and more than five thousand Sisters. In the last thirty-five years of her life, Mother Teresa traveled from one house, one country, or even one continent to another on average every third day. More than five thousand elaborate, theological-spiritual letters have emerged. But she would probably say about all of it, "Everybody can do it." The important thing was something else—how she did it.

On her tomb, on the ground floor of the Motherhouse of the Missionaries of Charity in Calcutta, is a verse from chapter 15 of the Gospel of Saint John: "Love one another, as I have loved you" (Jn 15:12).

23

Mother Teresa Lives!

MOTHER TERESA lives on—with the Lord, of course, whom she served her whole life long, but here and now as well, through her Sisters. Over and over again I have had the privilege of witnessing, on different continents and in different countries, how very much alive Mother Teresa's spirit is in the religious family that she founded.

Even during her lifetime, many people in Mother Teresa's inner circle worried about how the work would continue after her death and who would be able to direct it. Her standard reply was, "If God managed to begin this work with such nothingness, then it will not be difficult for Him to find someone who will continue it better than I. It is His work."

～

Interestingly, the official miracle that the Church approved as the basis for Mother Teresa's beatification was not performed for a Catholic. The Indian woman who was miraculously cured was an animist (a person who believes that spirits inhabit non-human entities). After several unsuccessful courses of treatment, she was in the final stages of cancer and came to the Sisters' house to die. The Sisters prayed with her and asked Mother Teresa to intercede. The woman fell asleep. When she woke up the next morning she was—as the doctors later confirmed—completely cured.

Years ago, the Sisters in a large Brazilian city told me about a strange encounter. They regularly visited families and elderly people who lived alone in one of the *favelas* (slums) where not even the police dared to go. The area was ruled with cruelty and violence by local drug mafia. One day a young man knocked on the door of the Sisters' house. They did not know him, but they invited him in.

He stayed where he was and then, turning to leave, said, "I am from the *favela*. Yesterday I broke a drug mafia law. Tomorrow I will be dead. No one can protect me."

"Can we help in some way?" asked one of the horrified Sisters.

"No, I wanted to come to you on my last journey, to tell you that I'll be dead tomorrow. You are probably the only people in the world who would be interested."

To try to help the people in the *favelas*, the Sisters first set up a copy of the Pilgrim Virgin Statue of Our Lady of Fatima at the edge of one of the slums. An enormous crowd of children immediately gathered, and the Sisters prayed with them. When they had finished praying, the Sisters asked, "Whose family most urgently needs the Mother of God?"

A little girl spoke up and said that her mother was now all alone and had been acting very strangely. The Sisters went to her home and met a woman who was clearly psychologically disturbed. Only at the little girl's insistence did the mother even let the Sisters in. But then she told her story. The drug mafia had set fire to her husband and hung his charred body on her front door. A little later they had kidnapped her son, cut his body into pieces, and left them in front of her door.

The Sisters taught the woman the Hail Mary and left the statue of Our Lady of Fatima with her for nine days. When they visited again, the room had already changed; everything was suddenly clean and neat. The woman was psychologically sound. "The Mother of God has healed me, but you can't take her away from me," she said.

Of course the Sisters left the statue of Our Lady with her. Today the woman is one of the Sisters' coworkers.

In Buenos Aires, the capital of Argentina, the Sisters look after a poor neighborhood. One day they heard shots a few blocks away. Undeterred, they walked toward where they had heard the shots. A man they knew, clearly drunk, staggered toward them screaming, "Now I'll kill her!" (presumably his wife), and gesticulated wildly with a revolver. Everyone else ran away to safety; the Sisters walked straight up to him, took the revolver out of his hand and said, "Don't be silly. Now come and lie down in your bed."

Mother Teresa's courage clearly continues to affect the way the Sisters behave. In Phnom Penh, the capital of Cambodia, the Missionaries of Charity run a house for AIDS orphans and also a program to feed the poor. They had a large warehouse in which they stored donated items and, one night, it was robbed. The Sisters woke up, walked to the warehouse and discovered the guard they had employed masterminding the theft. He was standing there with a loaded gun, guarding the thieves as they carried off the food. The superior walked straight up to him and ordered him to put everything back.

"No closer, or I'll shoot you!" he screamed.

"Good, either shoot me now or put everything back," the superior replied, showing no sign of fear.

The result? He had his men put everything back.

Soon after the end of the terrible killings in Cambodia in the 1970s, the Sisters in Phnom Penh started to take in AIDS patients who had been thrown out by their families because of their illness. These unfortunate people simply wandered the streets as long as they could find something to eat; when their meager supplies ran out, many took their own lives. Later the Sisters also took in HIV-infected children who could not stay with their parents. They sent them to school and gave them the most up-to-date medication, with the result that their life expectancy increased by sixteen to eighteen years. Once, when I was spending a few days there, I noticed an emaciated but radiantly cheerful girl who was one of the HIV-infected children—the only one who regularly came to morning Mass.

While leaving the Sisters' house one day, I saw this girl being driven out in a car through the main gate. She rolled down the window and called to me, as if giving me the best news of the day, "Father, today I'm going to the city for my last check-up. Then I'll come back here to die." With her radiant smile she waved to me until her car disappeared from view.

The Sisters in Armenia told me another story. One night in the dead of winter they heard a noise in the house. When one of the Sisters went to the entrance to see what it was, she saw a masked man. He seized her, held a large knife to her throat and yelled, "Give me all your dollars!"

She answered, "We don't have any!"

"Roubles, then!" demanded the burglar.

"We don't have any roubles in the house, either."

Finally the man said, "Then pack up something for me to eat!"

So the Sisters packed spaghetti, jam and whatever they happened to have in the kitchen for him to take with him. They thoughtfully also included salt and utensils. As soon as everything was packed, the man grabbed the bundle of food out of the Sister's hand and ran out the way he had come in. He had broken in through the main door and walked through the chapel to the Sisters' residence. Now, running out through the chapel again, he suddenly turned and said, "Your God will never forgive me!"

A Sister replied, "Yes, He will, if you ask Him for forgiveness."

The man turned to leave and said to the Sisters, who were shivering in the cold, "You must close the door behind me."

But he had damaged the door while breaking in and it would not close. When he saw the Sisters' helplessness, he had them bring a hammer and began to mend the door. As soon as it was mended, he took his package and ran away.

I am quite sure that those Sisters prayed a lot for their burglar, that he might recognize that their God—Who is also his God and the God of us all—will gladly forgive him, if only he opens his heart to accept God's forgiving love.

These, and many other signs of extraordinary love, testify that Mother Teresa lives on today—in heaven, of course, even though she once said, "I will be absent from heaven so as to help on earth." In heaven, too, it is her heart's desire "to give many saints to Holy Mother Church" and "to fill heaven with the poorest of the poor from the slums." And meanwhile, here on earth, she continues her work through her Missionaries of Charity and all the good that they do.

After Mother Teresa's beatification, Cardinal John Patrick Foley said, very astutely, "Anyone who wants to see Blessed Mother Teresa today need only look at her Sisters." As with

Mother Teresa, one sees in them the "pencil of God," through which He enables us to experience His love, even today. Today, through their devotion to the poorest of the poor, they too proclaim Jesus.

The best Catholic content.
All in one place.